Telepathy for Beginners

The Psychic Development Guide to Telepathic Abilities

© **Copyright 2023 - All rights reserved.**

The content contained within this book may not be reproduced, duplicated, or transmitted without direct written permission from the author or the publisher.

Under no circumstances will any blame or legal responsibility be held against the publisher, or author, for any damages, reparation, or monetary loss due to the information contained within this book, either directly or indirectly.

Legal Notice:

This book is copyright protected. It is only for personal use. You cannot amend, distribute, sell, use, quote, or paraphrase any part, or the content within this book, without the consent of the author or publisher.

Disclaimer Notice:

Please note the information contained within this document is for educational and entertainment purposes only. All effort has been executed to present accurate, up-to-date, reliable, and complete information. No warranties of any kind are declared or implied. Readers acknowledge that the author is not engaging in the rendering of legal, financial, medical, or professional advice. The content within this book has been derived from various sources. Please consult a licensed professional before attempting any techniques outlined in this book.

By reading this document, the reader agrees that under no circumstances is the author responsible for any losses, direct or indirect, that are incurred as a result of the use of the information contained within this document, including, but not limited to, errors, omissions, or inaccuracies.

Free Bonus from Silvia Hill available for limited time

Hi Spirituality Lovers!

My name is Silvia Hill, and first off, I want to THANK YOU for reading my book.

Now you have a chance to join my exclusive spirituality email list so you can get the ebooks below for free as well as the potential to get more spirituality ebooks for free! Simply click the link below to join.

P.S. Remember that it's 100% free to join the list.

~~$27~~ **FREE BONUSES**

- 9 Types of Spirit Guides and How to Connect to Them
- How to Develop Your Intuition: 7 Secrets for Psychic Development and Tarot Reading
- Tarot Reading Secrets for Love, Career, and General Messages

Access your free bonuses here
https://livetolearn.lpages.co/telepathy-for-beginners-paperback/

Table of Contents

INTRODUCTION 1
CHAPTER 1: IS TELEPATHY REAL? 3
CHAPTER 2: LEARN TO MEDITATE FIRST 13
CHAPTER 3: RAISE YOUR VIBRATION 23
CHAPTER 4: NURTURE YOUR CLAIRS 34
CHAPTER 5: ESTABLISH A TELEPATHIC BOND 43
CHAPTER 6: LISTEN TO OTHER'S MESSAGES 51
CHAPTER 7: SEND MESSAGES TO OTHERS 59
CHAPTER 8: EXERCISE YOUR TELEPATHIC MUSCLES 67
CHAPTER 9: HEAL THROUGH TELEPATHY 73
CHAPTER 10: RAISE YOUR TELEPATHIC PROTECTIONS 84
CONCLUSION 94
HERE'S ANOTHER BOOK BY SILVIA HILL THAT YOU MIGHT LIKE 96
FREE BONUS FROM SILVIA HILL AVAILABLE FOR LIMITED TIME 97
REFERENCES 98

Introduction

Telepathy is the ability to receive and deliver thoughts and feelings to and from another person, regardless of the distance between you. This process is done without involving any of the five senses of smell, sight, touch, hearing, or taste. Telepathic communications can only occur between people operating on similar levels of consciousness. This means that the closer the person you have in mind is to you, the more successful your efforts will be.

You may be surprised to learn that we are all blessed with the gift of telepathy. We just have to know how to nurture and develop it correctly to establish telepathic connections with others. So many people are unaware of this possibility because they're usually highly skeptical or even ignorant. One sure way to block off all psychic tendencies is by doubting this power or your ability to perform telepathy effectively, which is definitely not a good start. Telepathy only works if you trust that it's possible and have faith in your ability to send and receive messages in this way.

Learning to tap into another person's consciousness can significantly improve all your relationships. It helps you to understand and relate to people better, and it becomes easier to deal with others when you can read them like an open book.

You can also extend your telepathic connection to other living beings, such as animals. Imagine being able to intuitively feel your pet's wants and needs at all times. Since animals are more sensitive to potentially dangerous situations, you can pick up on their anxiety in good time to protect them and yourself from imminent hazards.

When reading this book, you'll learn everything you need about telepathic communication. It is the ultimate psychic development guide to awaken your psychic abilities. It is perfect for those who are entirely new to the subject and individuals who have some knowledge about psychic development but are looking to develop telepathy in particular.

This guide is a comprehensive and interesting journey into the art of telepathy. It is easy to read and comes with hands-on methods and instructions on nurturing skills like mind-reading and sending mental messages to others. Here, you will find out how to establish a telepathic bond with anyone you have in mind. You'll learn how to be open and receptive to other people's telepathic messages and recognize signs that someone is already trying to mentally communicate with you. You'll come across exercises that will help you improve your focus and concentration skills, which will help you throughout your telepathic endeavors.

This book will also teach you how to use telepathy to send positive and healing energies to others. You'll find numerous exercises and meditation techniques to help you channel and direct healing energy toward a specific person. Finally, you'll learn how to identify when someone is sending or attempting to send you negative energy or even feeding off your energy. The last chapter provides detailed instructions on effectively protecting yourself against these energetic attacks.

Chapter 1: Is Telepathy Real?

In the X-men movies, Professor X's superpower is reading people's minds even over a great distance. He also can project his thoughts into the minds of other mutants and people's minds. As you have seen from the movies, he can communicate telepathically even with those who don't share his gift. He can also control others, which makes him powerful and, at times, dangerous. People watch these movies and wonder if this superpower is real or just the product of the writer's imagination. Movies tend to exaggerate and amplify simple gifts, turning them into superpowers for dramatic effect. Although superpowers aren't real, skills are, and you can develop any skill you want with the right training and hard work.

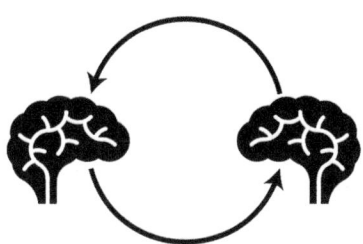

Telepathy isn't just a beautiful and unique gift. It can also be very helpful.
John C. Osborn, CC0, via Wikimedia Commons:
https://commons.wikimedia.org/wiki/File:Telepathy_(26882)_-_The_Noun_Project.svg

Unfortunately, there are various misconceptions about telepathy; we will dispel these a little later. In real life, telepathy is different from how it is portrayed in movies. To start off with, it isn't a superpower, nor is it dangerous. It also doesn't let you control other people. This is a good thing because you don't need the burden of a superpower and end up being chased by bad guys all the time. Real telepathy allows you to communicate with others using thoughts rather than words.

In this chapter, you will learn about telepathy, its history, and the scientific research that backs it up.

What Is Telepathy and How Does It Work?

Movies like Star Wars and X-men may have given you an idea of what telepathy is like. However, it is best to forget everything you have learned about telepathy from the media and look at the topic from a fresh perspective. Telepathy is the ability people can develop to communicate with each other using their thoughts. Instead of the mouth, with telepathy, the mind does the talking. In other words, telepathy is a non-verbal and non-physical form of communication. You don't need to use any of the five senses; it is simply a direct communication between minds. People can send thoughts to one another even when they aren't in the same room. For instance, you may think of one of your high school friends and then receive a phone call from them the next day. When you were thinking of your friend, they picked up this thought and acted on it by calling you. Have you ever called a friend or a family member and they tell you, "I was just thinking about you. This is crazy..."? Well, it isn't crazy; in some cases, it is no coincidence. This could be telepathy at work.

So, to answer the main question here, yes, telepathy is real. There is a type of ability called extrasensory perception or ESP that is usually exchanged and perceived without using the five senses. Psychics, clairvoyants, and telepaths all use ESP. There are still people who regard telepathy as a farce or something that Hollywood has invented. However, the science behind telepathy has proven these people wrong. In fact, it isn't just human beings that can use telepathy but animals, like monkeys, use it too.

It is best described as the activity of the brain's nerves, which emit electrical signals transmitted as messages, allowing people to communicate with each other. Scientists have discovered that they can read these signals using advanced electronic devices. They placed electrodes on top of the heads of a group of volunteers to record the brain's electrical activity. However, these signals pass through the brain membranes, the skull, and the skin. This may have impacted the accuracy of the results, but this is one of the few methods scientists use to understand how telepathy works.

So now that they had witnessed these signals, the next step was to decode them. This can be tricky because brains have their own language, which is "thought." Scientists got their volunteers to produce electroencephalography activity. For instance, the same type of electrical brain activity is released when you think of moving your arms. With further study, the scientists could recognize a few patterns in the thought process. So, volunteers were asked to focus on specific thoughts.

The next step was to transmit these thoughts to another person's head, which is the act of telepathy. Scientists transmitted the thoughts through electrodes. Other methods don't require using wires. They used certain devices to create a magnetic field to facilitate the transmission of thoughts. A volunteer focused on a specific thought that the researchers read as electroencephalography activity, which was transmitted through a magnetic field created by a TMS (Transcranial Magnetic Stimulation wand). This stimulated the brain of another volunteer, and they began seeing flashes of light.

This experiment was conducted at the University of Barcelona. As complicated as it sounds, it helped scientists to see that thoughts could be transmitted from one person to another, thus proving telepathy is real. Despite the science, did we really need experiments to prove that? If you watch your day-to-day life closely, you will notice that you have been communicating your whole life telepathically. People use their brains to send messages to each other all the time.

Telepathy can be viewed as mentally influencing another person's mind. Simply put, a person can think of a specific thought to make another person think the same. The first person is aware that their thought is a message meant to influence someone else. This isn't meant to exert control over someone. On the contrary, it could be used to help them or even ask for help. For instance, you broke down in the middle of nowhere, and your phone battery died. You can telepathically bring someone to where you are by using telepathy and influencing their thoughts. This is a type of telepathy called MOBIA, which stands for "mental or behavioral influence of an agent."

In other cases, the receiver is the one who is aware of the telepathy instead of the one sending the thought. For instance, when someone is waiting to get news or certain information, they can meditate or focus on the news they are expecting, so when they get a thought or image in their mind, they are aware that this is the message they were waiting for.

Telepathy isn't just a beautiful and unique gift. It can also be very helpful. You may find yourself in a situation where you want to say something but find yourself unable to put your thoughts into words. Or maybe you want to reach out to someone, but you don't know how to take the first step or what you'll say to them. In this case, you can communicate your thoughts by allowing your higher self to take charge and deliver the message you are struggling with. In fact, there are emotions so deep and raw that they are better expressed telepathically rather than during a conversation. A good example of this is getting closure after a breakup or forgiving someone. This type of message can have a deeper meaning when sent telepathically.

Nervousness can sometimes take over, and many wish they had a skill to help them during these situations. Telepathy, properly developed, can become the trait you rely on when you are in need. If you are new to telepathy, it will help you think of it as a sixth sense or a second language you can use. For example, you speak French, and you meet a French person who doesn't speak a word of English. In this case, you will speak to them using your second language instead of French because this is the only way you can communicate with them. The same applies to telepathy, as it is a language that you can use when there is no other way to communicate, and unlike French, telepathy is a universal language.

Types of Telepathy

There are different types of telepathy that you need to know about before you start to tap into your telepathic gift.

Mental Telepathy

Mental telepathy, also referred to as "thought transference," is a type of telepathy where two people communicate with each other using their minds. In other words, it is about transferring thoughts between two individuals. Concentration is key with this type of telepathy. The two people involved must be focused and conscious of the telepathic process.

In the eighth century, there was a Buddhist master called Padmasambhava. He studied various Buddhist practices and brought them to his home in Tibet. He wanted future generations to benefit from his teaching; He decided to employ mental telepathy to transmit his teachings to other Buddhist masters. This way, he could guarantee that his teachings wouldn't be lost, and each generation of masters would pass them down to the next.

Author Alice Ann Bailey, who worked closely with Tibetan masters, believes that in a couple of hundred years, most people will communicate using mental telepathy. This is a sentiment that Facebook founder Mark Zuckerberg also echoed.

Instinctual Telepathy

Instinctual telepathy isn't as strong as mental telepathy. In fact, it is considered one of the weakest forms. Animals and humans use this type of telepathy, and some cultures still use it. Instinctual telepathy allows a person to pick up on someone else's needs or feelings. The person doesn't have to be nearby to signal these needs. This type of telepathy works at a distance, and for it to be effective, one must employ their solar plexus chakra, which is located in the stomach area and is responsible for emotions and instinct. According to Hawaiian priests, people can communicate telepathically through their solar plexus. They believe the subtle body of a person, the invisible energetic field that surrounds every person, sends an invisible thread to another person's solar plexus, connecting both people. They then can communicate telepathically using these threads.

A person doesn't receive the telepathic message right away. You first receive the message instantly, and then, the instinct transfers it to the rational part of you, which then delivers it to the mind, which processes it like a memory. The more two people communicate telepathically using this "thread," the stronger their connection becomes. The threads of both people braid with each other to create an unbreakable bond. You can easily send out threads to others just by shaking hands or looking at each other.

In Africa, people use a different method of instinctual telepathy. In the Kalahari Desert in South Africa, people believe that there is a stream of energy, often silver, that connects all living beings with each other. The solar plexus also plays a role here since the stream of energy stretches out from the belly button. Think of these streams as phones with each person on a line and communicating with one another.

In Australia, some cultures believe in the "Miwi," which allows them to see and hear things from a distance. "Miwi" is located in the solar plexus chakra, which means instinct or soul. People get this gift from their parents, and they pass it down from one generation to the next. There are also cultures in Japan that use the solar plexus to communicate instinctively.

The west also has a term for it, and that's a "gut feeling." People call it the inexplicable feeling they get in their gut about a situation or person. You have probably experienced this feeling on more than one occasion. You may have felt that someone couldn't be trusted based on a gut feeling or decided that your gut swayed you toward it. In their day-to-day life, everyone makes decisions based on their instinct, and even detectives will follow a lead based on a hunch or a gut feeling.

In 2004, Parapsychologists Marilyn Schlitz and Dean Radin conducted experiments to prove that people can communicate telepathically using their gut feeling. The test subjects were all couples, and each couple was separated into different rooms. In one room, Radin and Schlitz showed one person different pictures that evoked emotions. The other person was placed in a different room with electrodes and was monitored. They found that the person in the second room responded to strong emotions evoked by the first person, which proved that the gut feeling has its own brain and perceptions.

Spiritual Telepathy

Just as the name suggests, spiritual telepathy involves communicating from one soul to another. It is the highest form of telepathy, requiring the soul, brain, and mind to be aligned. This will allow you to mediate between the spiritual and physical worlds. It allows you to reach enlightenment and access information provided by the divine. This information can help you solve problems in the physical world and help others as well. In fact, one of the greatest artists of all time, Leonardo da Vinci, believed that a painter's mind is inspired by the divine and that if the spirit wasn't involved, he would not be able to produce art. Michelangelo also believed that the divine was the source of his creativity. This belief was illustrated in his painting "The Creation of Adam." In the painting, God is depicted in what looks like the human brain and extends his hand to a man who represents divine inspiration.

The History of Telepathy

The concept of telepathy is nothing new. Ancient cultures like the Greeks and Egyptians believed in telepathy. The ancient Greeks believed that they could communicate with others through dreams. The ancient Egyptians also shared the same thoughts about dreams. They believed that spirits are able to communicate and send each other messages in dreams. This is probably why ancient cultures took their dreams so seriously because they believed they meant something.

Psychologist, F.W. Myers, was the one who coined the term "telepathy" in 1882. Myers was one of the people who helped form the Society of Psychical Research. During that time, significant research was carried out on the topic of physical sciences. Great advances in this field paved the way for scientists to dig deeper into the topic of mental phenomena. They were hoping to make sense of certain paranormal phenomena. As a result, the term "telepathy" came into being, with Myers working to prove that telepathy is real.

Zener Cards Experiment

Throughout history, scientists have always been curious about telepathy and have worked to find proof that this intriguing concept is real. J. B. Rhine, the founder of parapsychology, came up with an experiment to test for telepathy. This experiment was called "the Zener cards experiment." Rhine used five cards, each with a different shape: a cross, a square, a star, three wavy lines, and a circle. However, this experiment wasn't Rhine's first attempt to navigate the world of telepathy. He first used to play cards with volunteers, who were mostly students. The volunteers would try to guess which card the researchers were holding. However, the results of this experiment weren't accurate, as people weren't really guessing but were suggesting their favorite cards instead. Rhine wanted to get more precise results, so he came up with the Zener cards. The idea was to choose shapes the volunteers weren't connected to or associated with. The experiment was named Zener after the involvement of Rhine's friend, psychologist Dr. Karl Zener. It was Zener who came up with the five shapes because he believed that most people wouldn't be biased toward any of them. Naturally, chance played a role here, but a person wouldn't guess the right cards five or ten times by chance. This meant that there was a possibility that a person doing this was a psychic.

Rhine then decided to use the same method to test for telepathy. Two people were placed in different rooms, and one of them would look at each of the cards. This person would then try to send an image of each card to the person in the next room using telepathy. The person in the other room would try to guess the image communicated to them. The more a person was able to guess the card, the clearer it was that they were gifted. For instance, if someone guessed right 15 or 20 times, they were no longer guessing. They were, in fact, using telepathy to communicate with one another.

The Ganzfeld Experiment

Parapsychologists conducted this experiment to further prove that telepathy is more fact than fiction. Volunteers were asked to wear a paper mask with the edges taped. A red light was turned on and filled the room, ensuring it *didn't* flicker. This was intended to cause sensory deprivation. No noise was allowed in the room except for white noise. One person was placed in this room, while the other was placed in a different one. The person in the normal room was asked to focus on a picture. Meanwhile, the other person would describe the hallucinations they experienced in the red light room. If their experience was the same as the picture the other person was focusing on, then both people were communicating telepathically, and this experiment was a success.

CIA Investigation

In the '70s, the CIA investigated the concept of telepathy to spy on the Soviet Union. In 2017, classified information came to light that showed the CIA had a program that was called "Project Star Gate." The CIA was looking for people who had special gifts like telepathy or psychokinesis. They sought the help of the famous psychic Uri Geller. They hoped to take advantage of his telepathic powers and learn how to read other people's minds. The analysis of the results of this experiment was very hopeful in proving that individuals can indeed have paranormal abilities.

Telepathy and Quantum Physics

There is a theory that suggests that telepathy and quantum physics are connected. The theory postulates that the brain can receive and influence "quantum fluctuations" from other people's brains. According to Albert Einstein, all humans are connected to this universe, and the idea that we are separated from one another is an illusion. As a result, people can communicate with each other using telepathy. This theory also echoed how many cultures believe people can connect with each other using a stream of energy or an invisible thread.

Can Anyone Be a Telepath?

Telepathy is a skill, and just like any other skill, you can learn it and develop it with time. Anyone can be a telepath, but this isn't something that will happen overnight, nor will it give you the same powers as Professor X. With time, learning, and training, many may be able to send and receive messages using their minds.

FAQs

Is telepathy dangerous?

No, telepathy isn't dangerous. It is simply a form of non-verbal communication that can influence thoughts to allow you to communicate with someone or ask for help.

Can anyone practice telepathy?

Yes, anyone can practice telepathy. It is a skill that you can develop over time if you train and work hard.

Is everyone born telepathic?

Yes, everyone is born telepathic. However, it can become rusty when you ignore your gift or stop paying attention to it.

Will I become a telepath once I start training?

Not right away, but you will get better with time and practice.

Is good health associated with telepathy?

Yes, being healthy is necessary to be able to communicate using your mind. When you are sick, your body, mind, and soul weaken, which can influence your telepathic abilities.

How do I know that my message has been sent?

You will know in your gut that your message has been sent. It's a feeling you'll get inside that your thoughts have reached the other person's attention. You can then stop communicating and wait for the reply.

How do I know someone is communicating with me telepathically?

You will think, feel, imagine, or have certain desires toward something. Don't ignore these feelings, as they may mean someone is telepathically trying to communicate with you.

How will telepathy help me?

Connecting with others on a higher level allows you to better understand and relate to them and their struggles. This can improve your relationships and help you establish strong bonds.

We are all connected, and no man is an island. You may be getting telepathic messages, but maybe you aren't aware. As a result of skepticism and the stereotypes surrounding telepathy, most people see the messages as coincidences or think they imagined things. Open your heart and mind to the universe and give yourself a chance to be at one with it and all its beings.

Chapter 2: Learn to Meditate First

Suppose you want to learn how to develop your telepathic abilities. In that case, the first step is *believing* it is possible. Telepathy, also known as "mind reading," is the ability to communicate with others without using words or any other physical means. It is a natural ability that we all possess, but most of us are unaware of it – or do not know how to use it.

A crucial step in your training to develop your telepathic ability is to learn how to meditate.
https://www.pexels.com/photo/woman-meditating-in-bedroom-3772612/

The good news is that telepathy is a skill that can be learned and developed with practice. This chapter will cover the basics of telepathy and how you can start using it in your everyday life.

Believe in Yourself

The first and most important step in learning telepathy is to believe in yourself. We all have the ability to communicate telepathically, but many of us block it out because we don't believe it is possible. Ask yourself why you want to learn telepathy. What are your motivations? Focusing your energies and developing your abilities will be easier when you have a clear purpose.

Start with baby steps. Do not try to force a telepathic connection but just let it happen naturally. The more you practice, the stronger your abilities will become.

Be Open-Minded

To be a good telepath, you need to be open-minded. This means being receptive to the thoughts and feelings of others. It also means being willing to share your own thoughts and feelings with others. When you are open-minded, you will find it easier to establish a telepathic connection with someone.

Be with Someone You Trust

When starting out, it is best to practice with someone you trust. This could be a family member, friend, or even a pet. Choose someone open-minded and receptive to the idea of telepathy. Once you have established a connection with this person, you can start practicing with others.

Create a Relaxing Environment

To be successful, create a relaxing environment. This means being in a quiet place where you will not be interrupted. Make sure that you are comfortable and not feeling rushed. Focusing your energies and establishing a connection will be easier when you are relaxed.

Focus on Your Intentions

When you are trying to establish a connection with someone, focus on your intentions. This means having a clear purpose for why you want to connect with this person. It will also clear your mind so you can open up the channels.

Let Go of Your Ego

To be successful in telepathy, you need to let go of your ego. Stop trying to control the situation or the other person and open yourself up to the idea that you might not always be successful. When you let go of your ego, you will find it easier to establish a connection.

Practice Visualization

One of the best ways to develop your telepathic abilities is to practice visualization. This means picturing yourself sending and receiving messages to and receiving them from another person. Visualize the other person clearly, and see yourself communicating with them.

You can also try to send a specific message to the other person. For example, you could focus on sending the word "Hello" to them. See the word clearly in your mind, and then let it go. Trust that the other person will receive the message.

Telepathy is a skill that takes time and practice to develop. Do not get discouraged if you do not see results immediately. Remember to believe in yourself and be open-minded; you will eventually start seeing results.

Meditation and Telepathy

A crucial step in your training to develop your telepathic ability is to learn how to meditate. Meditation will help clear your mind and focus your thoughts, two essential components of successful telepathy. If you've never meditated before, don't worry - it's not as difficult as it seems. This chapter will teach you the basics of meditation and explain how to get started.

What Is Meditation?

Mediation is an ancient practice used throughout history to help people achieve complete mental and physical well-being. In its simplest form, meditation is a way of clearing your mind and focusing your thoughts. When you meditate, you allow yourself to become fully present in the moment and let go of all distractions. This helps you relax or de-stress and improves your focus and concentration.

Different types of meditation all share the same basic goal: to make peace with the mind and allow you to focus on the present moment. Some common types of meditation include mindfulness, transcendental, mantra, focused, and guided meditation.

Hinduism and Meditation

Meditation is central to Hinduism, one of the world's oldest religions. Hindus believe it can help you connect with the divine and lead to inner peace and enlightenment.

All types of meditation involve focusing the mind on a single object or thought. This can be done by sitting quietly and focusing on your breath or by repeating a mantra (a sacred word or phrase).

Pranayama in Hinduism

Pranayama is a type of breathing exercise often used in meditation. It helps to calm the mind and control the breath, two important components of successful meditation.

Pranayama is usually done by sitting comfortably and focusing on the breath. The breath is then slowly exhaled through the nostrils, and the process is repeated.

To do pranayama, sit with your spine straight and close your eyes. Place your hands on your stomach, and inhale deeply through your nose. As you inhale, feel your stomach rise. Then exhale slowly through your mouth. Repeat this process for several minutes.

Yoga and Meditation

Yoga is also an ancient Indian practice that combines physical exercises, breathing techniques, and meditation. Yoga can help to improve your flexibility, strength, and balance, as well as calm the mind and relax the body.

Yoga is often used as a tool for meditation. The physical postures and breathing exercises help to focus the mind and prepare the body for meditation.

To get started with yoga, find a class or video suitable for your fitness level. There are many different types of yoga, so you can choose a class that is right for you.

Start by doing a few minutes each day, and gradually increase the amount of time you spend practicing. Yoga is a great way to prepare your body and mind for meditation.

Guided Meditation

Guided meditation involves someone else guiding you through the process. This can be done in person or by listening to a recording.

Guided meditation is a great way to learn how to meditate if you are a beginner.

There are many different types of guided meditation, but they all have one thing in common. They help you to focus and direct your attention. This is helpful, particularly if you have difficulty meditating on your own. Guided meditation can also be used to explore specific topics or areas of focus, such as relaxation, stress relief, or self-compassion.

If you are interested in trying guided meditation, many resources are available. You can find guided meditation recordings online or at your local library. You can also take a class or workshop or participate in a meditation group.

Hinduism teaches that the goal of meditation is to still the mind and experience the true nature of reality. This process is known as nirvana, which is said to be the ultimate goal of life.

Meditation is not easy, but it is worth the effort. The benefits include improving your mental and physical health, having more peace of mind, and experiencing a deeper connection with the divine.

If you're interested in trying meditation, many resources are available to help you. You can find books, classes, and retreats that will teach you how to meditate.

It is essential to find a method that works for you and stick with it. Meditation is a journey, not a destination. There is no one right way to meditate, so find a method that feels comfortable and that you can continue for as long as you want to meditate.

How to Meditate

Now that you know a little about meditation, it's time to learn how to do it. The good news is that anyone can learn to meditate, regardless of experience or ability. Just follow these simple steps:

1. **Find a relaxing place to meditate**. You can meditate indoors or outdoors, in a quiet room, or in the midst of chaos. The only requirement is to find a spot where you can comfortably relax without being disturbed.
2. **Gently close your eyes and take deep breaths.** Relax your whole body and clear your mind of all thoughts. As you inhale, focus on filling your lungs with fresh air. When you exhale, let

all the tension and stress of the day disappear.
3. **Begin to focus on your breathing.** Pay attention to the sensation of your breath as it enters and exits your body. Notice the rise and fall of your chest or stomach as you breathe.

If you can't focus for extended periods, that's okay. Meditation is not about clearing your mind completely - it's about learning to focus despite the presence of distractions.

Continue focusing on your breath for as long as you like. When ready to wind it up, take a couple of deep breaths and get up.

Meditation Tips for Beginners

Here are a few tips to help you get the most out of your meditation practice:

Don't Expect Miracles

Meditation is a tool, not a magic wand. It will take time and practice to see the benefits. Start with just a few minutes a day. You can gradually increase the time you meditate as you get used to it.

Be Patient

Meditation is a journey, not a destination. There is no need to rush. Meditation is not a race, so there's no need to try and clear your mind completely in one sitting. Just start with a few minutes a day and work your way up from there.

Practice Daily

Meditation takes practice, so don't get discouraged if it's difficult at first. It takes time to learn how to keep peace of mind, but you will eventually be successful with patience and persistence.

Find a Comfortable Position

You don't have to sit in a lotus position or anything like that - just find a position that you can comfortably maintain for the duration of your meditation.

Set a Timer

Set a timer when you meditate, so you don't have to worry about how long you've been sitting there. Just choose a comfortable length of time (5-10 minutes is a good starting point) and let the timer do the rest.

Stay Consistent

The more you meditate, the better your results will be. So, find a time you can guarantee you can stick to and set it aside as an unbreakable appointment with yourself. Even a few minutes of meditation daily can make a big difference.

With these tips in mind, you're ready to start meditating! Just remember to be patient and go at your own pace. Meditation is a journey, not a destination - so enjoy the ride.

Benefits of Meditation

Meditation has a host of benefits for both the mind and body. Here are just a few of the ways that meditation can improve your life:

Reduces Stress

Meditation has been shown to be an effective way to reduce stress. It can help to calm the mind and body and promote relaxation. In Hinduism and Buddhism, meditation is used to help people achieve enlightenment. With regular practice, it can help to improve your mental and emotional well-being.

Improve Focus and Concentration

Meditation can also help to improve focus and concentration. One study found that those who meditated were better able to focus on a task and had improved memory recall. In addition, meditation has been shown to increase activity in the parts of the brain responsible for attention and focus.

Improved Sleep

Meditation can also help to improve your quality of sleep. Meditating for 20 minutes before bedtime improved the quality of sleep and speed of falling asleep compared to people who did not meditate. In addition, they were less likely to wake up during the night.

Mental and Physical Health

Meditation has also been shown to improve mental and physical health. People who meditated had lower levels of anxiety, depression, and stress. They also had a better immune function and improved cardiovascular health. Meditation has also been shown to reduce pain perception.

Increased Creativity

Meditation can also help to increase creativity. This is because when you meditate, you are training your mind to be more open and flexible. This means that you will be better able to come up with new ideas and solutions to problems. Also, because meditation can help to increase focus and concentration, it can help you to execute your ideas better.

So, meditation is a great way to do it if you want to increase your creativity!

Enhanced Self-Awareness

Meditation can also help to enhance self-awareness. This is because it lets you quiet the chatter of your mind and focus on your thoughts and feelings. This can help you to better understand yourself and your needs. In addition, self-awareness can help you to make better choices in your life.

Improved Emotional Health

Meditation can also help to improve emotional health. This is because it helps to reduce stress and anxiety. In addition, it increases positive emotions such as happiness, love, and compassion. Meditation can also help you to deal with difficult emotions such as anger, sadness, and fear.

Expanded Consciousness

You will find your consciousness is expanded, and you can tap into o a higher state of awareness when you meditate regularly. You will be more connected to your inner thoughts and feelings in this state. You will also be more aware of the world around you. This can help you to better understand yourself and your place in the world.

Stepping Stone for Telepathy

Not only does meditation have all of these great benefits, but it can also help to improve your telepathic abilities. This is because meditation hones your focus and concentration. With regular practice, meditation will help you to develop your telepathic abilities.

How Meditation Improves Telepathic Ability

Regarding meditation and psychic abilities, there is a common misconception that to develop psychic ability, one must have been born with some sort of supernatural gift. This could not be further from the truth! In fact, meditation is one of the most effective ways to improve your telepathic ability.

How Does Meditation Work to Improve Telepathy?

When you meditate, you train your mind to focus and be more aware. With regular practice, you will find that it becomes easier and easier to focus your mind on a single thought or object. As your ability to focus improves, so does your ability to tune into the thoughts and feelings of others.

Telepathy is all about energy and vibration. Everything in the universe vibrates at a certain frequency, and our thoughts and feelings are also made up of energy. When you focus your mind during meditation, you are raising your own vibration and becoming more attuned to the vibrations of others. This makes it easier to tune into their thoughts and feelings and communicate with them deeper.

As well as improving focus, meditation helps to still the mind and to quieten the mental chatter, which is essential for clear communication. It also helps to open up your third eye chakra, which is responsible for psychic abilities. A calm mind is a more receptive mind, and a more receptive mind is better able to receive telepathic messages.

Another way meditation works to improve telepathic ability is by expanding consciousness. As your consciousness expands, you will become more aware of the world around you. This includes the thoughts and feelings of others. With regular practice, you will find that it becomes easier and easier to tune into the thoughts and feelings of others.

When you are physically and mentally healthy, your telepathic abilities will also be stronger and more reliable. That's why it's so important to take care of your body and mind – and to meditate regularly. Meditation will clear your mind and reduce stress and anxiety. It will also help you to connect with your higher self and to access your intuition and inner wisdom.

Finally, meditation helps to increase your overall energy and vibration. The higher your vibration, the easier it is to connect with others on a psychic level. When you meditate regularly, you will find that your vibration gradually begins to rise, making it easier for you to connect with others telepathically.

You will be able to send and receive messages more clearly, and your abilities will continue to develop as you meditate more. So, if you want to improve your telepathic ability, add meditation to your daily routine! The more you meditate, the stronger your telepathic abilities will become. Just like any other skill, it takes practice and patience. But with regular meditation, you will find that your ability to communicate telepathically will improve greatly.

Meditation is a powerful tool that can be used to improve telepathic ability. By training the mind to focus and be more aware, you can tune into the thoughts and feelings of others more easily. Meditation also helps to still the mind and to open up the third eye chakra.

In addition, it helps to expand consciousness and to increase your overall energy and vibration. The more you meditate, the stronger your telepathic abilities will become.

Chapter 3: Raise Your Vibration

High vibrational frequency can help you easily send and receive messages via telepathy. In this chapter, we'll explore vibrational energy and why raising your vibration is necessary to communicate successfully. You'll understand the link between vibration and telepathy and recognize signs that show you whether you have a high or low vibration. Finally, you'll find tips on raising your vibrational frequency.

High vibrational frequency can help you easily send and receive messages via telepathy.
https://www.pexels.com/photo/silhouette-of-man-at-daytime-1051838/

What Is Vibrational Energy?

Everything in the world is composed of energy. Even our bodies are made of vibrating particles that generate energy. You may be surprised to learn that some healthcare approaches, like vibrational medicine, use the vibrational energy that the patient's body creates for healing.

Vibrations are rhythmic. Some of these rhythms, like the changing seasons, take place on a large scale. Others occur within our bodies. The breath we take, circadian rhythms, and heartbeats are just a few examples of rhythms you can measure. However, there are also countless other minuscule vibrations happening inside our bodies. For instance, the molecules within each of our cells are constantly vibrating. Some vibrations are smaller than 0.001 of the diameter of just one of your hairs.

Together, these vibrations create waves of electromagnetic energy, impacting how your body functions and triggering changes inside your cells. Not all molecules vibrate at the same rate. They can be either slower or faster, depending on the body temperature and other internal and external conditions.

Our behaviors, thoughts, and feelings can influence the rhythms and vibrations in our bodies. For instance, negative emotions, like anxiety, trigger the release of cortisol, a stress hormone. This hormone may cause the heart rate to speed up. Music also generates vibrational frequencies. These will interact with our energetic fields and induce changes in the body. This is why listening to calming music can help you get your heart rate to slow down. The vibrations emitted by external sources impact our emotions, thoughts, and body function.

Vibrations generated by our thoughts and behaviors can also change the smaller rhythms in our bodies. You can change the vibrational speeds of the atoms in your body by changing your environment, taking control of your emotions, managing your thoughts, and being mindful of your actions. Since electromagnetic energy travels in waves, influencing changes in your body's nano vibrations can ripple further, creating changes in your overall mental and physical well-being.

Why Is It Important to Raise Your Vibration?

Raising your vibration is among the best ways to nurture your spiritual, mental, emotional, and physical health. The process of raising your vibration is a lot easier than you think it is. However, before we get into that, let's explore why you would want to raise your vibrations.

Eliminates Negative Energy

It works to get rid of negative energy. It helps you create a space for yourself where thoughts, objects, attachments, imprints, and people with low vibrations and low densities can't function. Having low vibrational energy makes you vulnerable to the negativity of others. Other people's words and behavior can easily influence your mood and emotions. Having low vibrational energies can even put you at risk of being susceptible to spells and curses. However, take charge of your energy and always maintain a high vibrational frequency. You will be untouchable to undesirable vibrations. We only interact and resonate with vibrations that match our own, meaning that anything beneath your energy will not be considered a part of your reality.

Helps You Manifest Abundance

This also means you'll be able to manifest abundance into your life easily. You're already vibrating on the same energetic frequency of everything you want. Being more focused and aligned with your desires can help you make them a part of your reality.

Gives You a Sense of Direction

Maintaining high vibrational frequencies can give you a sense of direction and control in your life. Instead of being subject to the dynamics of the world around you and letting yourself be affected by undesired situations, thoughts, and feelings, you can control what your energy interacts with. Being able to bring your desires into reality changes you from a secondary character in the world to the narrator of your own story.

Increases Your Spiritual Awareness

Eliminating lower vibrational frequencies from your life can also help you with your spiritual endeavors. Since higher vibrational frequencies mean fewer intrusive thoughts and blockages, you can focus your attention on becoming more spiritually aware. You'll learn how to optimize your thoughts and feelings to be more balanced internally and with the world around you.

Helps You Foster Deeper and More Energetic Connections

Raising your vibration expands your aura and makes your energy more powerful. It increases the energetic space you take up in the world, making it easier to cultivate deep connections with everything around you. This makes you more grounded and aligned with nature and the universe around you. It teaches you to stay in the present moment, reminds you to express your gratitude toward Mother Earth, and gets rid of unwanted thoughts. Raising your vibration is the hardest part. Maintaining your effort, however, is relatively easy because your vibrational energy is a self-filling cup. Gratitude, a positive mindset, and being grounded can help you further elevate your vibrational frequency.

Enhances Your Spiritual Gifts

Since a higher vibrational frequency means stronger energetic connections and fewer internal blockages, you can expect your spiritual gifts to be improved. You can enhance your four clairs of intuition (which include clairaudience, clairsentience, claircognizance, and clairvoyance) by raising your vibrations, which enhances your telepathic effort. You may even discover that you possess new spiritual gifts that you knew nothing about before you raised your vibration.

Allows You to Feel Empowered

Feeling empowered is one of the best feelings in life. Nothing has the same effect as knowing exactly what you want in life and understanding what you're capable of. Think of what our brains and energies can do; we are very powerful beings. Raising your vibrations can help you realize this, meditate on how connected you are to the universe, and learn your role in the world. Being spiritually aligned and fostering a positive state of mind can help you to achieve your personal development goals.

Makes You More Compassionate

With higher vibrations, you'll find you feel generally happier, which makes you become more compassionate. You start giving out more love and positive energy to everyone around you. Sending love out to the world is one of the most healing gifts you can give to those around you.

Boosts Your Overall Well-Being

Low and negative energy makes you feel depleted and flat. Diminishing these emotions makes you feel more energized and increases your vitality. Maintaining high vibrational energies makes you more driven and attentive and increases your vitality. It elevates your overall well-being and sense of self.

Vibration and Telepathy

Raising your vibrations is essential when it comes to telepathic communications. Increasing your vibrational awareness automatically makes you more intuitive, which, in turn, enhances your psychic powers. Being highly intuitive improves your claircognizant (clear knowing), clairsentient (clear feeling), clairvoyant (clear seeing), and clairaudient (clear hearing) senses, which allows you to communicate more effectively using telepathy. We will explore the clairs in more depth throughout the following chapter.

A higher vibrational frequency also allows you to tap into other people's energies more effectively. You can communicate telepathically with someone only when you have a similar vibrational frequency. You can't tune into a person's consciousness if they have a higher vibration than yours.

Keeping your vibrational energy high also protects you from unwanted intrusions by negative energy. You're vulnerable to their fears, ideas, and thoughts whenever you tap into someone's consciousness. Maintaining high frequencies allows you to release everything that isn't yours.

Do I Have a Low or High Vibration?

The higher your vibrations, the more you experience positive feelings and qualities. People with high vibrational energies are generally more peaceful, loving, compassionate, and forgiving. In retrospect, suffering from low vibrational energies leaves you with a plethora of negative and unwanted feelings and emotions like hatred, regret, greed, and fear. Those with low vibrational energies are prone to develop conditions like depression, anxiety, and other physical ailments.

High vibrations make you more attuned to your higher self, consciousness, and universe.

Take a moment to think about who you truly are. What are you without your interests, knowledge, belongings, passions, personality, feelings, and thoughts? Would you cease to exist if all your memories and experiences were stripped away from you? No. You'd still have your consciousness. Raising your vibration can help you connect with this elemental aspect of yourself or your true nature.

The lower your vibration, the more you lose touch with who you are and your highest self. This makes your life experiences more challenging.

Before we explore the signs that you have a high or low vibration, there are a few things to keep in mind. There is no black or white regarding who or what you are. You can't have 100% low or high vibrations. You'll always fall somewhere on a spectrum, whether that is 20% low and 80% high, 65% low and 35% high, and so on. This is why you should always avoid labeling yourself as one or the other.

You should also remember that understanding your vibrational frequency is meant to be good for you and not give you an excuse to label others. Unfortunately, many people tend to segregate others with low vibrations once they understand what energy is. It's good to protect yourself from energy vampires and negative individuals. However, instead of cutting these people off and advising others to stay away from them, you can maintain your own vibrational frequency by practicing meditation and gratitude and keeping a positive mindset.

Signs You Have a Low Vibration

- You feel stuck in life
- You don't have a clear sense of direction
- You're not empathetic toward yourself or others
- You're emotionally disconnected
- You have quick and intense emotional reactions
- You always feel tired and lethargic
- You have ego-centric tendencies
- You've been told that you think the world revolves around you

- You find it impossible to leave old or unhealthy habits behind
- You never feel fulfilled
- You have a pronounced shadow self
- You argue with others a lot
- You struggle with poor life choices
- You always feel guilty about something. Even if you aren't, you find yourself searching for something to feel guilty about.
- You complain frequently
- You find forgiveness challenging, whether it's toward yourself or others
- You can't see the beauty in life
- You're in constant despair
- You don't know what you want in your life
- You have self-sabotaging tendencies
- You're often very skeptical
- You usually feel jealous or resentful
- You eat a lot of processed and unhealthy foods
- You eat an unbalanced diet
- You find it hard to feel gratitude
- You're physically unhealthy
- You've been told you're needy
- You demand a lot from others
- You consume a lot of violent media content (music, video games, movies, books, etc.)
- You always focus on the negative things in life
- You always feel like a victim
- Your relationships always bring you pain
- You struggle to make progress in any area of your life

Signs You Have a High Vibration

- You have high self-awareness. You are conscious of your actions, words, feelings, and behaviors and realize their impact on others.
- You're emotionally balanced. Your emotional reactions don't blow out of proportion.
- You know when to take yourself seriously and when to let loose
- You often nurture yourself and others
- You're attuned to your body and its needs
- You're generally empathetic. You are sensitive to the needs of others and try to see things from their perspective.
- You feel connected to something greater than yourself
- You find it easy to experience joy and happiness
- You approach life with ease and a sense of humor
- You're self-disciplined
- You realize that you don't need something or someone else to be happy
- You generally feel strong, energetic, and healthy
- You don't struggle with patience
- People find it easy to open up to you
- You live in the present and don't spend too much time dwelling on the past or worrying about the future
- You don't feel the need to start arguments or get the last word in
- You're confident in yourself and your capabilities
- Forgiveness toward yourself and others comes easily to you
- It feels like you know what you want to do in life. You've found your calling.
- You have a strong intuition

- You are often the adviser, teacher, or peacemaker in your friend group, and all your relationships
- You usually experience synchronicities
- You often feel or express gratitude for all that you have
- You're able to delay gratification and pleasure when you know it's not in your best interest
- You try to lead a clutter-free life
- You are open to new experiences, people, ideas, and beliefs
- You're very creative and inspired
- You eat a balanced diet
- You eat raw and unprocessed food
- New opportunities come to you easily
- You don't experience much disappointment in your life. This is because you don't attach yourself to relationships and habits that don't serve you.
- You understand that "passing things," like people and material items, are temporary, which is why you don't cling to them
- You like to consume inspirational and relaxing content (music, TV shows, movies, books, etc.)

How to Raise Your Vibration

Raising your vibration is not a difficult endeavor like many assume, but it requires time, effort, and patience.

You often have to change your lifestyle to raise your vibrational energy. The extent of these alterations depends on your current habits. If you smoke and eat takeout daily, you'll have to put in more work than those who don't.

Letting go of your unhealthy habits and getting used to the changes in your life is perhaps the hardest thing about raising your vibration. However, once you get the hang of it, you'll realize that it's the best decision you've ever made. You'll elevate many aspects of your life in the process.

Before starting this journey, you need to understand that raising your vibration is not a one-time process. If you don't keep up your effort, your energetic frequency will fall again.

Here are some things you can do to raise your vibration:

Practice Gratitude

This is the simplest thing you can do to raise your vibrational energy. Negativity is your worst enemy - it is detrimental to your physical, mental, emotional, and spiritual health. Make it a habit to name three things that you're thankful for as soon as you wake up in the morning and before you go back to sleep. Think about all the great things that you receive in your day and take them for granted.

Try to change your perspective about your life's "negative" aspects. For instance, if you wish to find a less tiring job, try to change your thinking instead of resenting it. Be thankful that you have a job that allows you to pay your bills. This isn't an invitation for toxic positivity or guilt-tripping yourself. The aim is to recognize your life's blessings and express gratitude toward them, no matter how big or small.

Meditate

Incorporating meditation into your daily routine can be a great way to start your day or blow off some steam before you go to bed. Meditating helps you let go of intrusive thoughts and relieve anxiety symptoms. It helps you connect with yourself and the world around you. Practicing meditation regularly trains your mind to think positively and is a great way to lift your mood and vibrational frequency.

Surround Yourself with Nature

Break away from the hustle and bustle of life and go for a long walk in nature. You can also consider keeping a few plants at home and caring for them. Nature has a calming effect on the mind and body. It can ease symptoms of depression and anxiety and reduce cortisol levels in the blood.

Practice Positive Thinking

Negative thought patterns are habitual, and habits are hard to break. However, you should take small steps toward adopting a positive attitude. Remind yourself that everything in life happens for a reason, and trust that the universe is always working in your favor, as this can help you respond to undesirable situations more easily.

Be Around People Who Make You Feel Good

As mentioned above, working toward raising your vibrational frequency is not an excuse to segregate those with lower vibrations. However, you should take precautions whenever you're around negative-minded individuals. Consciously take control of your emotions and thoughts, and be careful not to absorb any energies which aren't yours. You should also aim to spend time with people who make you feel good. Spending time with individuals with higher vibrations can help you raise your own.

Try to Be Generous and Forgiving

You will struggle to adopt positive characteristics like forgiveness and generosity if you have a very low vibrational frequency. The rewards, however, are worth your effort.

Eat a Healthy and Balanced Diet

The food you consume also influences your vibrational frequency. Lower your meat, processed food, fried food, and alcohol intake as they have low vibrational frequencies. Making healthier food choices elevates your energy.

Raising your vibrational frequency has numerous benefits for the mind, heart, soul, and body. It empowers you, gives you a sense of direction in life, makes you more thankful and compassionate, and, most importantly, enhances your spiritual gifts. Becoming more intuitive can help you communicate telepathically more effectively. It also ensures that you don't accidentally absorb thoughts, feelings, and behaviors that aren't yours in the process.

Chapter 4: Nurture Your Clairs

As you've probably gathered from what you've read so far, intuition plays an essential role in telepathy. So, what better way to develop this skill than trusting the intuitive guidance coming from your senses? Telepaths rely on their ability to use their extrasensory gifts - known as the clairs. The four clairs are the fundamental pillars of your psychic powers, and honing them is an enormous step forward toward becoming a successful telepath. This chapter will introduce you to the clairs and offer valuable advice on developing the two most prominent ones - clairvoyance and clairaudience. These two reveal themselves in pictures or spoken worlds, both of which can send powerful messages to a telepath.

Intuition plays an essential role in telepathy.
https://www.pexels.com/photo/woman-doing-hand-gesture-over-a-white-moonball-8770811/

The Clairs

If you use Tarot cards, runes, or other forms of intuitive practices, you may have already had a chance to use the clairs. For example, you may have had instances when you just knew the meaning of the card, rune, or any other tool as soon as you picked it up. You may not have even started thinking about it, but you already know what they're telling you at that moment. Or, even if you don't practice any of these, you may have been pondering about an issue that had you worried, and suddenly, you understood and have an answer to the situation. You sensed, heard, saw, or knew something that helped calm you down and found a solution to your issue. If yes, you've received intuitive guidance through one or more clairs.

The four clairs are clairvoyance, clairaudience, clarcognition and clairsentience. Most people are born with at least one of these senses, but not everyone is aware of them. Yet anyone can develop and tap into them, which is great news for telepaths. However, only a few people have an instinctive ability to tap into these senses. Most people have to actively work on sharpening them. The first step in connecting with your clairs is acknowledging them. This allows you to let your guard down and let them guide you intuitively toward changes or whatever path you've chosen for yourself. If this path is being a telepath, all the more reason to take the time to understand how your clairs can empower your physic abilities. The clairs can teach you how to be empathetic with your intuition. And by showing how your intuitive decisions can benefit you, they'll encourage you to trust it enough to let you make decisions.

Not only that, but through the clairs, you can pick up messages, understand the guidance and recognize other forms of wisdom you may telepathically receive. Whether you want to consult with spirits and other enlightened beings or communicate through your telepathic abilities, the clairs will be the perfect tool for it. The spirits and other beings may prefer communication in a particular way, and a heightened intuition will pick this up. The clearer your Clair senses are, the more likely you'll be able to receive and decipher these messages correctly. Understanding and nurturing your clairs will help you to uncover your values and establish your identity as a telepath. They'll teach you what works for you in your psychic practices and what you can do to elevate them to a higher level.

Clairvoyance

Despite being the most common of the clairs, clairvoyance is probably the most misunderstood. While most people know that clairvoyants can see things others are unaware of, it goes far beyond this. Clairvoyance is essentially a psychic's third eye - and this is even truer for telepaths. Whether you receive a subtle visual message like a flash of color, experience vivid premonitions, or detailed visions depends on many factors. Psychic seeing is different for each person experiencing it because everyone has ingrained patterns which contribute to how they perceive information. Some mediums can even visualize messages from the past, depending on how they receive messages. Others describe the information they receive popping up as (for them well-known) symbols. In modern times, people have also referred to clairvoyance as seeing messages in a window, just as one would on a widescreen TV, computer, or mobile phone. You may also get clear visions of someone trying to warn you about something that is coming in the future. Or a person with a distinct trait appears and serves as a reminder of something you need to do in the present. The messages you receive through this clair are metaphors. For example, if you see someone carrying a large backpack, this may indicate that you're bearing a heavy burden. Whereas, if you see the earth moving beneath you, this may mean you feel that your life is unstable and you're standing on shaky ground.

Clairaudience

The other form of information telepaths rely on is auditory messages. These are spoken words you get through clairaudience. The words that come through are intuitive messages that sound similar to your voice - especially if you hear them in your head. It's also possible to sense them with your outer (normal) hearing, in which case they often sound like a different person's voice. Whether you know this person or not, you'll be able to clearly distinguish their voice. Besides thoughts, clairaudients can also hear music - not to mention sounds that may sound like they're coming from this world and some that come from the spiritual realm. With sufficient practice, you can make the acoustic messages louder and clearer. Just like their visual counterparts, the auditory signals also vary in clarity. Sometimes, they can be as clear as your own voice, coming through as a short and straightforward message. For instance, you may hear a voice telling you that you should wait until you receive a promotion before purchasing a car. At other times, they'll come through unfiltered and require a little patience before you understand their point. For example, you can hear someone telling you very loudly that you must stop controlling your life. In this case, you'll need to examine in which area of your life you need to loosen control.

Clairsentience

Clairsentience is the sense that relies on tactical stimuli. In most cases, the message will take the form of a physical reaction to something you do or experience. For example, you're viewing a picture of a frozen landscape, and you suddenly start feeling cold. Or you touch someone's hand and suddenly feel they are about to experience something unusual. These sensory experiences are all characteristic of clairsentients. While they rarely impact telepaths directly, these tactile messages represent the perfect way to sharpen your intuition. They teach you how listening to intuition can lead to extraordinary information. Sometimes, instead of pointing out something you were aware of in your gut, clairsentience will tell you that something isn't as it is supposed to be. This is another form of intuitive insight, a visceral sensation that if you don't change your currency course of action, you can expect trouble in the future. The messages can come off as positive or negative emotions, symptoms of illnesses, and even physical injuries. Sometimes the source will be clear, whereas, at other times, you'll have to put in more effort to find out where the message comes from. For example, you may experience pain, fear, and other uncharacteristic emotions related to a place, a situation, or an event. Or you'll feel the energy shift inside your body - and you'll have to figure out why it happened. You may also be able to read the emotions of others. This may come even easier than understanding your feelings - especially your gut feeling.

Claircognizance

Sometimes a medium doesn't even have to see, hear or feel a message. They'll know something is true or needs to be done. It just appears in their mind as intuitive wisdom without being backed up by rational thoughts. This is called claircognizance or psychic knowing, another indirect factor that may affect telepaths. Sometimes, the message will be a strong awareness that something is wrong or an insight you need to focus on in your psychic power. Either way, you'll know the information you've received to be accurate simply because your intuition tells you it is. You won't know how or why your gut urges on it, but you won't question it either - which you'll probably do at the start of your journey until you decide to use the wisdom you receive to guide you. Telepaths may also use claircognizance to develop their telepathic abilities further. Simply having your gut feelings to back you up can make you more accurate during your psychic work. It's also worth mentioning that it's one of the most efficient channels you can use for communication. After all, you won't have to focus on hearing, seeing, or sensing anything. You just have to listen to your intuition, and you can have the information in your mind in a matter of seconds. Let's say you have a complex relationship with someone. Because of this, you can't decide how you feel about them. You can tap into your gut feelings and discover you have a bad feeling about this person.

Developing Your Psychic Senses

Most mediums have a preferred way of receiving psychic messages. They may be sensitive to all forms, but one of them will always be more influential. After some practice, you may be able to tune into several clairs. However, at the beginning of your journey, you should focus on only one form of extra sensory stimuli. Telepaths will typically need to nurture clairvoyance (physical seeing) or clairaudience (psychic hearing). Tuning into these can increase your awareness of your higher self. It'll also give you a different perspective for observing your intuition and allow you to practice and sharpen your telepathic abilities.

Developing Clairvoyance

Developing clairvoyance may sound easy, but it's probably the hardest one to master. You need to be attuned to potential visual messages, which is only possible if you tap into your intuition. Once you've conquered that, your clairvoyance skills will become more powerful, and the messages will become clearer.

Non-Verbal Communication with Your Intuition

Everyone is born with intuition. However, most people stop relying on it because of different societal rules, expectations, professional pursuits, or the stressful nature of day-to-day life. If this is the case with you, working with your intuition will be just as strange and awkward as seeing a friend you haven't seen in years. Your subconscious will have memories of your working together. However, the dynamic of your relationship has changed over the years. And although you are both the same people as you were before (literally), you and your intuition may as well be complete strangers. To work together again, you'll need to renew your relationship. To do this, stop from time to time and devote a couple of minutes to getting to know your intuition, as you would with a childhood friend. Ask questions frequently to learn how you can work together in the future. These don't have to be overly reflective questions but simple inquiries about your inner feelings. A great exercise for this is color-coding your emotions and asking your intuition to help identify them. For example, think about a recent experience - maybe a frustrating conversation you've had with a friend. Let's say you've assigned the color yellow to frustration. When asking your intuition, it will pick it up easily because you already have this information in your conscious mind. Over time, the color will be linked to the emotion subconsciously, which will come in handy next time you need to identify the feeling. Let's say you had a similar experience with someone else and aren't sure about the feeling it caused you. When tapping into your intuition, you need to ask it to show you the color of your emotion. If you suddenly see the flash of yellow, you'll instantly know you're frustrated.

Surveying and Predicting Your Environment

Scanning your environment is another great way to cultivate clairvoyance. To do this, sit or stand in the middle of a room or larger space. If you're standing, start moving around and look for potential signs in your environment. You can also do a quick survey with your eyes if you're sitting. Pay attention to all the sights. Is there any particular one you feel drawn to? Perhaps something you find appalling? Make sure to look into every corner and piece of furniture you can see from your position. As awkward as this exercise sounds, you've probably done this many times before when you were in an unfamiliar setting, waiting in line, or wanted to avoid an uncomfortable conversation. You just weren't aware of doing it. Practicing it consciously will help you familiarize yourself with your surroundings, so you can pick up subtle visual signs. Eventually, you'll be able to use these skills to explore settings you don't know well. This is the next step in learning to use clairvoyance. Once you can confidently use the clair to explore familiar settings, you can consider visiting a place you haven't visited before. Close your eyes and set an intention of seeing the place in question. This will prompt your mind to visualize it. Memorize how you've imagined the place to look (you can also draw or describe it in a few lines to help you retain the memories). Go there physically, and compare your vision to reality. See how many shapes and positions you recognize. If you find a few that look very familiar, you are on the way to developing sharp clairvoyance skills.

Dream Analysis

Yet another way to access psychic seeing is by exploring your subconscious through dreams. When you're awake, your mind may limit how many visual signals you can receive. This is because absorbing more would threaten your ability to live a balanced and functional life. However, the information you haven't been able to store in your consciousness may still reach you but get tucked away in your subconscious instead. Dreams often symbolize an alternate reality - one in which you can see and experience more. They allow you to move more freely - and explore your environment and access the full potential of your extrasensory gifts. To do this exercise, before going to bed, set an intention of what you want to explore in your dreams. Place a pen and paper on your nightstand and go to sleep. Falling asleep, you'll tune into your fluid subconscious. When you wake up, think about everything you've seen in your dreams, and draw or write down any sight you feel is relevant.

Developing Clairaudience

Clairaudience is much easier to develop than clairvoyance, yet people often aren't aware of having this ability. However, if you prefer learning through auditory signals, love listening to music, talking to yourself, and giving advice to people after listening to them, you may already have the innate ability of clairaudience. Here are a few ways to link your intuition to this skill and sharpen them both.

Listen to Your Environment

The easiest way to reveal your psychic hearing skills is to practice listening to the sounds in your environment. This will make your physical hearing more sensitive and allow you to pick up auditory messages subconsciously. To do this, you'll only need to close your eyes and start paying attention to sounds you don't usually focus on. If you're outside, this may be the sound of leaves rustling under your feet or people talking around you. Tune in to the different sounds and focus on them for a short time. The more you practice this, the wider your hearing range (both physical and psychic) will be.

Ask for Messages

Once you've learned to pick up simple sounds, you can start asking for specific auditory messages. Consider a question that has been occupying your mind lately. Ask this question or anything else you may want to learn from a spiritual guide or simply from your gut. Keep your ear open for the response. It can come in any form - a song on the radio, a word you hear during a conversation – or even a random sound you hear on the street.

Meditation

Meditating with your intuition is another highly recommended way to nurture clairs. And meditating with specific auditory signals is particularly good for sharpening your psychic hearing skills. For example, you can listen to guided meditation, relaxing music, or any other soothing sound that widens your range of auditory experiences. You may also simply choose to listen to the sound of your own breathing. You'll need a tranquil spot, comfortable clothes, and a quiet and peaceful environment. Turn off your electronics and ensure you won't be disturbed by other sounds from your surroundings. Close your eyes and listen to the air traveling through your body. Note any particular sounds you hear and when you hear them next time, compare the two sounds and the respective emotions they evoke.

Disclaimer

Having the ability to use your extrasensory senses can be wonderful. At the same time, they can represent a challenge, especially for beginners. Hearing voices and seeing things can be scary because these senses are also associated with mental illnesses. In the beginning, you may start hearing or seeing things when you least expect them, not to mention how distracting it can be to work on these gifts in today's world when noise and visual pollution is all around us. If you aren't prepared for a message, you may think you're experiencing a symptom of mental illness. However, when you hear or see things due to a mental illness, you're not experiencing reality. You're experiencing a signal your subconscious conjured as an alternate level of understanding. Receiving messages through the clairs is different. These messages come from your own intuitive awareness. They are real - and you should feel better after accepting them. Once you fully acknowledge your gifts, you'll see how much value they can add to your life. When you elevate your awareness of your senses, you'll be prompted to listen to your intuition more and more. With enough practice, you'll be able to look forward to the following messages and explore how you can use your gifts in telepathy. However, if you keep experiencing confusion, insecurity, anxiety, or another symptom that can make you question your mental health, consult a licensed professional about them. Don't practice clairvoyance or clairaudience until you've worked through these issues and have ensured that you'll be able to keep your mental well-being in check.

Chapter 5: Establish a Telepathic Bond

A telepathic bond is a connection you develop with another person, often someone in your circle, like a family member, friend, or energetically close to you. To communicate with someone telepathically, you need to establish a connection or a telepathic bond between the two of you. As a beginner, having this bond will facilitate easy telepathic exchanges. Telepathy is about exchanging thoughts, so this process will naturally require you to focus on your thoughts. This connection is established on a higher level as it doesn't require verbal communication. As mentioned in a previous chapter, some cultures believe you can create a telepathic bond with someone just by shaking hands or exchanging glances.

A telepathic bond is a connection you develop with another person, often someone in your circle.
https://www.pexels.com/photo/adult-affection-beads-blur-371285/

There are various ways to help you establish a telepathic bond with someone. Meditation is often a very effective technique. You can sit in a quiet place, take deep breaths with your eyes closed, focus on your breathing, and visualize this person. You can also write their name on a piece of paper and meditate while holding this paper. Having an accurate image of the person in your head is essential while visualizing. Seeing that instinct is significant in telepathic abilities, you can rely on it and your gut feeling to guide you through this process. You will feel it in your gut when the connection is created.

Carefully choose who you bond with for this to work. As a beginner, you can't just establish a bond with a complete stranger. It's better to bond with people you are already familiar with - like your partner, parents, siblings, close friends, or anyone with whom you feel an energy connection. Look for people who you feel comfortable around. They are the ones who have positive vibes that lift everyone's spirits. You may also find yourself connecting with them on a higher vibrational level. You will experience emotions like excitement, joy, and gratitude. Find people who make you feel good about yourself and love yourself more when you are around them.

Competition can threaten your relationships and weaken your bonds with people. Choose people you don't constantly compare yourself to, and do not choose those with whom you feel ashamed or insecure around. Bond with people with whom you feel free to be yourself. Anxiety has become the disease of the age, and most people are concerned either with worries about the future or regrets from the past. However, there are always people who make you feel at peace when you are around them and who silence all your doubts - even the critical voice in your head. Connect with these people, the ones who keep you calm, the ones who make you happy and only focus on the present moment. You don't have to talk or do anything to have fun; you can sit quietly with them without saying a word and still feel comfortable and at ease. There are no awkward silences.

Sometimes you put your guard up and build walls around you either to protect yourself or because you cherish your privacy. However, some people make you take these walls down and let you become your truest and most vulnerable self when you are around them. You open up to them and can share feelings and secrets you haven't shared with anyone before. They make you feel heard and create a safe space for you to be yourself and share all your secrets, as you know that they will never judge you. These are the people you want to create a telepathic bond with.

You connect with these people on every level and trust them because you know they have your best interests at heart. They keep you balanced, and you feel your vibe with them on every level. Deep down, you know the people you want to bond with. It's an instinct that makes you feel connected with them on some level, whether it's spiritually or energetically. When choosing someone to bond with telepathically, ensure that they only bring positive vibes and feelings to your life.

Don't bond with negative people who want to cause you harm. Many energy vampires are out there and will only bring negativity to you. A telepathic bond involves exchanging thoughts, and you don't want negative thoughts in your head or in your life. Listen to your gut. It will tell you if you go off course and choose the wrong person.

Twins Telepathy

You have probably seen it in movies or heard real-life stories about twins sharing a telepathic connection. Twins' telepathy is when one twin knows what the other is thinking or feeling, even when they aren't in the same place. Twins already have a unique relationship with each other. They shared a womb and have the same genes, and, in the case of identical twins, they share the exact same features. Twins also share similar brain patterns, which scientists believe is the reason behind their telepathic bond. Both fraternal and identical twins share this bond. They have a natural understanding of each other's emotions and feelings. For instance, when a twin is in trouble, the other twin will feel in their gut that something bad has happened. It isn't just their emotional connection that is strong, but their physical connection as well. Some twins have also reported that they often feel a physical sensation when their twin is in pain or suffering from emotional distress. For instance, one twin can feel pain in their chest at the same moment their sibling is having a heart attack, or a twin can feel pain in their abdomen while their twin sister is giving birth.

Twins may also act in the same way even when they aren't together. For example, they may call or text each other at the same time, cook the same food, and buy the same clothes. This proves that twins are attuned to each other's thoughts and emotions and that they may know what the other person is going to say or even finish each other's sentences. In fact, even twins who weren't raised together still share some similarities that go beyond their physical appearance, which shows that twins don't have to be raised in the same home or environment to share a telepathic bond. Researchers believe that twins who aren't raised together may share an even more powerful telepathic bond than those who are raised together. They have also explained that some twins who are raised together may try to fight this bond. Each twin may want to find their own identity away from the other and express their own individualism. As a result, they may do things or act in a certain way just to be different.

The concept of twins' telepathy has been around for centuries and has fascinated people all over the world. French author Alexandre Dumas was inspired by this idea, and it was the theme of his novella "The Corsican Brothers." The novella was about twins who weren't raised together yet shared a telepathic bond. Dumas described this bond as if they both shared the same body. When one felt physical or mental pain, the other felt it as well. Dumas's wording is very interesting as this is how twin telepathic bonds often seem - like two souls sharing the same body and brain.

Twins grow up bonded, so it doesn't feel strange or abnormal to them. For this reason, they use it without thinking. They don't need to meditate or even try to establish a bond because it is already there and active.

Many real-life stories of twins' telepathic bonds go beyond eating the same dish at a restaurant. It can even save their lives. Gemma Houghton, a young girl who lives in Britain, shared her telepathic story with her twin. She has a fraternal twin sister, and one night as she was relaxing at home, she had a feeling that her sister was in trouble. Her sister was taking a bath, so Gemma went up to the bathroom to check on her. She knocked at the door and called her sister, but there was no answer. Gemma opened the door to find her sister unconscious underwater in the bathtub. Gemma's sister almost drowned as she suffered a seizure and passed out. Luckily, Gemma sensed her sister needed help, came to her rescue, and saved her life. The twins' telepathic bond saved Gemma's sister's life.

Another example is of twins who were referred to as the Jim Twins. Their story was so popular that it was covered in various publications and websites. Interestingly, the Jim Twins, who were male, weren't raised together and didn't know about each other. However, both men married two women who shared the same name, both adopted dogs, gave them the same names, and even named their children the same names. Skeptics may claim that this is nothing more than pure coincidence. However, there are things that are just too strange to be coincidences, and this story is one of them. It wasn't a single similarity; it included wives, pets, and children's names. This means that even though they weren't aware of it, these twins were telepathically bonded and attuned to each other's thoughts.

There was another story of a girl whose ankle suddenly started swelling for no reason, only to find out later that her twin sister had broken the same ankle. There was also a story of a man who said he experienced excruciating pain in his chest at the same time his twin brother had a heart attack. There is yet another story of twin brothers who were working in a woodshop when one of the twins heard his brother saying that he wanted sandpaper, so he handed it to him. Interestingly, the brother never said out loud that he wanted the sandpaper. He only thought about it, but the other twin could hear his brother's thoughts because of their strong telepathic connection.

There were other twin brothers who we'll call Twin A and Twin B. Twin A was on his honeymoon, and Twin B was with his wife in his home. There was a break-in, and Twin B was robbed. At the same time, Twin A told his wife to pack her bags as they had to go back now because he sensed something terrible had happened to his brother. Another story is of teen twins. One of them was working while the other was having fun with his friends. The second twin and his friends had an accident in the middle of nowhere with no cellphone reception. When they managed to get service, he found that his brother had called him, so he called him back to tell him about the crazy accident. The other twin answered the phone, freaking out and asking his brother if everything was okay. He told him that he strongly felt something was wrong, so he called his twin to check on him.

Another twin said that his brother was on vacation with his wife. When the twin on vacation experienced sunburn, the other one felt hot and extreme pain in his skin. A young woman said that one day she was at work and fainted for a few seconds for no reason. When she recovered, she received a phone call to go to the hospital. She found out later that her twin sister had passed away at the same time as she had fainted. There is also the story of a girl who went to get a blood test while her twin was at school. The one at school noticed a broken blood vessel in her arm. She found out later it was the exact spot her sister had had the blood test.

Twin telepathic bond isn't something that they establish with age. It has always been there. This was clear from the story of these toddler twins. Toddler 1 and Toddler 2 were two years old at the time. Toddler 1 was playing calmly at her aunt and uncle's home while her twin, Toddler 2, was with their parents. Toddler 2 got her finger stuck in the door and required stitches. Toddler 1, who was still at her uncle's home, began crying and screaming frantically. Her aunt and uncle tried to do everything to calm her, but she was hysterical and shaking. All of a sudden, she calmed down and stopped crying. When her parents arrived with her injured twin sister, the aunt and uncle told them of Toddler 1 crying and shaking. The parents were shocked because, at the same time, Toddler 2 was getting her stitches. However, this story is even stranger because Toddler 2 was calm and didn't cry or flinch. Even the doctors thought that this was strange. The parents, aunt, and uncle believe that Toddler 2 transferred her pain telepathically to Toddler 1.

Thousands of stories about twins experiencing a telepathic bond prove Dumas had a point. It can sometimes feel as if they share the same body and mind.

Meditation Techniques

As much as meditation is an effective technique to strengthen telepathic abilities, it can also help strengthen your telepathic bond with the people in your life. Practice these techniques with your partner, sibling, friend, or anyone with whom you want to establish a telepathic connection. Even if you don't have a telepathic bond yet, these techniques will help you create one. For these techniques to work, sit in a quiet room without any distractions.

Meditation Exercise 1
1. Sit in a comfortable position.
2. Bring a string of mala beads to meditate on and hold them while you also hold hands.
3. Chant OM at the same time.
4. Each of you should move a bead with every OM sound.
5. Repeat the OM while breathing 25 times. Focus on your voice and breathing.
6. Next, focus on your partner's voice and breathing as they also chant 25 times.
7. Now, chant OM together.
8. Keep chanting until you finish the beads.
9. After you finish, chant OM one more time and feel the connection and bond between you and your partner.

Meditation Exercise 2
1. Sit in a comfortable position opposite each other.
2. Stare into each other's eyes.
3. Take slow and deep breaths while focusing on your breathing.
4. Feel the air as it comes in and out of your chest.
5. Keep focused on your breath, breathe slowly, and don't force it.
6. Keep doing this for a couple of minutes.
7. Next, you can begin the breathing exercise.
8. You or your partner can be the one who sets the pace for your breathing.
9. Take a deep breath and count to five.
10. Hold your breath and also count to five.
11. Breathe out while counting to seven.
12. Your partner should be following your breathing.
13. You both focus on each other's breathing.
14. Repeat the breathing exercise with your partner for five minutes.
15. Now, allow your partner to set the breathing pace.
16. Repeat the breathing exercise again for five minutes.

17. While breathing, make sure you take deep breaths, focus on your breathing, and keep staring at your partner.

Meditation Exercise 3

1. Sit in a comfortable position across from each other.
2. Close your eyes.
3. Breathe in and out deeply and feel your body relaxing.
4. Next, as you have relaxed your mind and body, open your eyes.
5. Stare into each other's eyes and focus on each other's breathing.
6. Now, as you look into their eyes, you will be able to see yourself in them.
7. You are no longer two individuals but two souls in one body.

Meditation Exercise 4

1. Burn scented candles around the room.
2. Sit opposite each other in a comfortable position.
3. Set intentions for what you hope to achieve from this meditation exercise - which is establishing a telepathic bond with your partner.
4. Close your eyes and set your intention. You can either repeat it to yourself or visualize it.
5. Now, create a telepathic connection with your partner. This connection can also be an emotional one. You can establish an emotional connection with them since this person is someone you trust and who is close to you.
6. Once you feel a connection is established, breathe in and out slowly.
7. Now, visualize there is a chord made of light flowing through you and them and connecting you together.

In a way, we are all connected, but some connections are stronger than others, while some bonds take time to establish. Creating a telepathic bond is possible with the people you love and care about because you already share an emotional connection. Believe that you can establish this connection, and let meditation guide you. If you are a twin, you are one of the lucky few with a telepathic bond with someone without even trying.

Chapter 6: Listen to Other's Messages

Telepathy is a two-way street. To communicate effectively with someone, you must be able to send and receive messages. In this chapter, we focus on the latter component of telepathy. You'll find out how to receive telepathic messages and read minds effectively. You'll also learn to recognize signs that someone is sending you telepathic messages and learn several mind-reading methods.

To communicate effectively with someone, you must be able to send and receive messages.
https://www.pexels.com/photo/silhouette-photography-of-people-2627060/

Reading Minds

Receiving telepathic messages requires you to hone your mind-reading skills. Believe it or not, we unconsciously try to read people's minds all the time. We spend a lot of time wondering why a person is acting a certain way, overthinking the reasoning behind their words, trying to understand their emotions, and wondering what goes inside this person's mind. The conclusions we reach are often based on our own intuition, which is powered by the depth of our connection with that person, and what we already know about them. We are always intuiting and observing other people's body language to find out whether they're engaged, bored, lying, tired, active, etc. We also try to anticipate their reactions to certain situations or news.

While reading minds from a psychic perspective requires more effort and consideration, you can benefit greatly from the type of mind-reading you do every day. This is why you should involve your consciousness and actively lean into your intuition in the process.

The following steps can guide you toward developing your mind-reading abilities:

How to Read Minds

Mind-reading requires a lot of time, effort, and practice, like every other skill. Your focus should be on practicing mindful thinking. Observing and reflecting on your environment and those around you can help you read minds more easily.

Step 1: Enter an Open and Receptive Mental State

The first thing you need to do is learn to let go of all your judgments. As scary as it may sound, you need to open yourself up to other people's energies and allow them to engulf you. Reading minds won't be possible if you can't accept and respond to others. Whether you're sending or receiving a message, you must realize that telepathic communications are mostly about the other person rather than yourself. This is the mindset and energy you need to approach this endeavor.

By keeping your mind and energy open, you'll be able to connect with other people's energy more effectively. It also increases your awareness and keeps you present in the moment. You can achieve this state of mind by practicing mindfulness, meditation, or breathwork techniques. Doing yoga is also a great way to ground yourself.

Step 2: Choose a Person

Psychic work always works best when you're focused on a specific intention. Selecting one person to work with will help you yield the best results. Once you choose a person, focus entirely on them. Visualize their face and imagine their features down to the last detail. Think of their posture, how they walk or stand, how they sound and talk, and their overall behavior and body language. Capture a mental image of the essence of that person.

Afterward, you need to separate the person in your mind from their surroundings. This can be hard to do at first, as you'll probably start replacing their actual environment with one of your own imagination. The key here is to eliminate any distractions in the background and focus only on them.

Step 3: Focus Harder

Now that you've separated the person from their surroundings, you need to move your attention to their face. Keep eye contact with them for 10 seconds. Holding your gaze for longer than that can make them uncomfortable, and anything shorter than 10 seconds won't let you connect effectively.

Break eye contact and start feeling the energy that you've drawn from them. Explore their thoughts, feelings, and emotions. You'll find that these things are already rushing into your mind.

Step 4: Deepen the Connection

After you get a sense of that person's energy, you need to work on deepening their connection. You're going to get a sense of what you wish to ask them after you gain insight into their thoughts. Allow this experience to guide the entire conversation. Keep in mind that these thoughts may be fun and nice or extremely dark and deep. Whatever they are, you have to maintain openness and receptiveness. Embrace these thoughts and discuss them with the person you're connected with.

Mind-Reading Tips

The greatest thing about learning to receive mental messages is that it requires you to boost your energetic flow, which you can do just by sharpening some of the skills that you already use daily. Mind-reading is significantly easier to develop than other psychic skills.

Here are some activities you can do to enhance your energetic flow and develop mind-reading skills:

Increase Your Emotional Intelligence

Being able to read a person's mind depends largely on your ability to read their emotions accurately. You can only do this if you have high emotional intelligence.

People who have high emotional intelligence:

- Read other people's body language
- Actively listen and reflect on other's words
- Listen to the person's tone and notice the way they speak

A person's tone of voice, body language, and attitude can tell you a lot about their feelings and what they truly mean. For instance, you can only tell if a person is being sarcastic or genuine through their voice and physical expressions.

Become a Better Listener

Many people don't realize that listening is a communication skill. It is actually the cornerstone of communication. If you think about it, you'll find that you often listen to other people to respond to them rather than to understand them.

Being understood is among most people's deepest desires. We all respond negatively when we feel overlooked. It makes sense that the other person will become closed off and non-receptive if you don't make an effort to understand their perspective.

Stay present and keep your mind from wandering whenever you're talking to someone. Listen to what they're saying and reflect on it. If listening is a vital life skill, it is the core of mind-reading.

Seek out Emotional Connection

While some people have very little empathy, we are all empathetic beings. Unfortunately, technological advancements have gone a long way toward diminished in-person communications, making it very easy to lose touch with our empathetic emotions. You should actively tune into your empathy by exploring your feelings. Once you're ready, try to focus on other people's feelings and consider how they understand and react to their own emotions.

Don't Jump to Conclusions

We always attempt to make sense of the world around us by making up stories - it's a human instinct. What do you do when someone sees your text and doesn't reply right away? Your brain probably comes up with a dozen different scenarios explaining why they left you without responding. You start wondering if you said something wrong, so you read your text over and over again at least a hundred times. To ease your anxiety, you tell yourself that perhaps they got into another fight with their family, which is why they didn't get the chance to reply. This made-up scenario, however, makes you worry even more. Then, you remind yourself of how busy their schedule is and how they probably forgot to get back to you.

Regardless of what the situation is and how reasonable you believe your assumptions are, you need to remember that you don't have enough information to form an opinion or conclusion. You don't know anything about their situation and intention, which means that your imagination has actually filled in most of what you think you know. The next time you make assumptions, remember to collect enough information before overreacting to other people's actions.

Signs Someone Is Sending You Telepathic Messages

Here are some signs that someone is trying to send you telepathic messages:

You Can Communicate Via Eye Contact

If someone is sending you telepathic messages, it can feel as if you're having a conversation with them whenever your eyes meet. This is because your eyes are used to communicating with each other. As explained in the exercise at the beginning of the chapter, you can subconsciously communicate your mood to a person. Experienced practitioners of telepathy can also guide a person's actions via eye contact.

You Receive a Psychic's Confirmation

If you suspect someone is trying to communicate with you telepathically, you can always get more clarity by consulting a professional psychic. Keep in mind that many "psychics," especially many of those who can be found online, are scammers. Use this as an opportunity to lean into your intuition. You probably shouldn't book another session with that psychic if something feels off.

Your Mood Swings Are Intense

Is your mood extremely unstable these days? Do you often alternate between periods of joy and sudden intense sadness? This may be your body's way of trying to deal with telepathic messages. For instance, if you're receiving a negative message, your body may translate it as sadness. The energies that these messages carry can affect your mood. Do you recall feeling disoriented and overwhelmed? This is likely a result of the information you're receiving.

They Interact with You in Your Dreams

Telepathic communications can also take place during sleep. If one of your friends appears in your dreams after a period of no contact, then they could be sending you telepathic messages. Recall as many details as you can, including how you felt during the dream. Think about how you felt when you woke up. The only way to determine whether this was an innocent dream or a communication attempt is to find out whether it is relevant to real life. If possible, talk to that person to find out whether your dream really carried a message. If you woke up feeling unsettled, then your friend may be telling you that they need your help. If it was a happy dream, then they may be excited to share joyful news with you.

Your Thoughts Are Attuned

If you feel that your thoughts are attuned to someone else's thoughts, it may be because you're telepathically communicating. For instance, your friend may sing a part of a song that was just stuck in your head, or they may say that they were craving pasta when you were just thinking the same. If you're communicating telepathically with someone, you can influence each other's thoughts.

They Are an Open Book

If you can easily tell what a person is thinking and how they're feeling, then you probably have an established telepathic connection. This is especially the case if this easy-to-read person isn't very close to you. You don't need to know much about a person's motivations, reactions, moods, and body language to be able to know what they're thinking and feeling if they're sending you telepathic messages.

Mind-Reading Exercises

If you're still not ready to tap into anyone's mind and read their thoughts, you can start by practicing with someone you trust. Incorporating mind-reading exercises into your routine can help you strengthen your intuition and will facilitate openness and reception. Keep in mind that you may not get the result you want straight away, so keep practicing. However, don't be discouraged. It takes time to be able to connect deeply with someone and completely trust your intuition to guide you throughout your interaction. The more you practice, the easier and more natural it will get.

These four simple exercises can train your mind to receive telepathic messages from others:

Have Your Partner or a Close Friend Ask You to Get Something for Them

Tell your close friend or partner that you'll pass by the grocery store after work. Ask them to clear their mind and relax. You can also ask them to do a simple meditation if they're willing. Once they're ready, they should mentally ask you to pick a specific item up from the store. They can visualize you doing it while repeating the statement to themselves multiple times before letting it go completely. When you go to the store, let your intuition guide you toward the item they requested. Try again if you don't get it right.

Ask Them to Send You a Mental Image

Sit quietly with your friend or partner. Focus on each other and assume that you're connecting with each other's minds. Your friend should imagine a certain image, such as a teddy bear. They shouldn't give you any hints about what they're thinking. Tap into the mental image that they're sending and try to intuit what it is. Get all your senses involved in the process. You don't necessarily have to see a teddy bear in mind, but you can sense things like comfort or softness.

Ask Them for Permission

Sit in front of your partner or friend. Touch your knees and hands together and maintain eye contact. Once you're settled, ask them for permission to read their mind. When they grant it to you, tell them something that you suspect about them. For example, you can say, "I suspect you haven't told me you received a new job offer." You must involve your intuition in the process because it will help you determine a suspicion that you believe is true.

Your partner or friend should repeat the statement back to you in a way that acknowledges it. For example, they can say, "I understand that you think I never told you I received a new job offer." They shouldn't confirm or deny the statement or add anything to it. You should be able to sense whether the statement is correct after hearing it from them. Ask them if your suspicion is correct. They should offer an answer and the needed clarification. Thank each other for your willingness to explore assumptions, and understand and listen to each other.

Guess Who's Calling You

Don't rush to see who's calling you each time your phone rings. Instead, take the time to tap into whoever is calling you. See if you already know who it is. You'll not get it right each time. However, the more you practice, the better the results you'll yield. Asking for confirmation from the person calling you can help you verify your guesses.

Mind-reading is not a special psychic ability that only the gifted can develop. Anyone can learn to read minds and receive telepathic messages from others. You can easily read other people's minds once you nurture your emotional intelligence, lean into your intuition, and work on your active listening skills. Chances are that someone is wittingly or unwittingly trying to communicate with you telepathically already. You can know for sure by watching out for the signs we mentioned above.

Chapter 7: Send Messages to Others

Now that you know how to be receptive to telepathic messages, we'll explore the other component of telepathy: sending messages to others. In this chapter, you'll learn how to communicate mentally with anyone, no matter how far away they are. You'll also learn to recognize a few signs that your messages have been successfully delivered to the person in mind.

Being able to send telepathic messages to others is a great tool, especially when you have something to say but don't know to do it.
https://www.pexels.com/photo/silhouette-of-man-sitting-on-grass-field-at-daytime-775417/

Sending Telepathic Messages

Sending telepathic messages to others is a great tool, especially when you have something to say but don't know how to do it. Sending mental messages also comes in handy when you want to talk about your thoughts and feelings, or reach out to an ex, even when it isn't the right thing to do.

Unfortunately, the dynamics of life, relationships, and communication aren't always easy - there will be times when you can't speak what is in your heart. This is why learning to work with your higher self to deliver these messages via telepathy can be of great advantage. Telepathic communications can help you get closure and forgiveness and deepen connections.

You may struggle to work out if you're communicating correctly at first. It's normal to feel anxious and even silly, as well. However, it helps to think about telepathy as a sixth sense that you're trying to rediscover. Developing your telepathic skills is similar to remembering an old instinct you have. Say you're a talented artist who hasn't drawn in years. You won't be able to draw portraits as perfectly as you once did the first few times around. You may not get the proportions right at all. With practice, however, you'll become more dexterous, and everything will eventually start coming back to you.

Telepathy is an instrument that connects you to the world around you. The best thing about this skill is that it can be nurtured and developed by everyone. We all have the ability to send mental messages, images, and ideas to others, but few people are aware of this possibility.

It's best to practice telepathy with someone that you already are strongly connected to, such as a close friend, family member, or partner. As you recall from the previous chapters, telepathic communication only takes place when you're vibrating on another person's energetic frequency. This means that you're likely telepathically communicating with them on some level, even if you don't realize it. A good place to start would be by paying attention to the mental interactions that are already taking place between you two.

Here is how you can master the art of sending telepathic messages:

Start in a Meditative State

Find an empty and quiet place to sit down. Get yourself comfortable and feel the tension leaving your body. Relax your limbs, jaw, and face muscles. Allow your shoulders to drop down. Empty your brain and visualize all intrusive thoughts flowing out of your brain. Once you enter a light trance state, start visualizing the person you wish to connect with. Envision them sitting or standing right in front of you as you send them feelings of gratitude or love. Imagine that these emotions are a form of energy that you can pass on to them.

Send Small Messages to a Loved One

You enter a deep trance state when you fall asleep, which is why it's possible to establish dream telepathic connections. To do that, ask your higher self for permission to access your highest consciousness to send someone a message before you go to bed. Use your thoughts to send a loved one a small message. Ask them, telepathically, to send their response to the message if they received it.

Be Open to Responses

If you do this correctly, the other person will likely call or text you the next day. They may mention that they've been thinking about you a lot recently or just felt the need to contact you or check on you today. If it's someone that you're no longer in contact with, they may reach out more subtly or passively. For instance, they may communicate with you on social media. Don't be discouraged if you don't receive a response. Sending telepathic messages can take a lot of time and practice to master. You should also keep in mind that you didn't necessarily fail if you didn't hear back from anyone. For instance, if you're dealing with an ex, they'll probably fight back the instinct to contact you.

Patience Is Key

Psychic endeavors require great levels of patience. Like everything in life, you can't be an expert overnight. You have to trust that you'll improve at your own pace. Telepathy also requires a lot of repetition, especially if you're new to the craft. You also need to understand that some people are better at sending messages than receiving them, and vice versa. Even though sending and receiving are both vital parts of telepathy, they require relatively different skill sets. It's okay to be naturally inclined toward one more than the other. You just need to identify which of them is your stronger suit so you can spend more time nurturing the other.

Reach out to a Mentor

Very few people realize the importance of maintaining good spiritual hygiene. Taking care of your spiritual wellness is crucial if you're working toward psychic development. Reach out to psychic mentors, book reiki healing sessions, and explore other holistic healing methods to cleanse your energy. You have to be very careful with telepathic communications because you're vulnerable to fears, thoughts, emotions, and ideas that aren't yours.

Sending Telepathic Messages from a Distance

Many people still don't fully understand the concept of telepathy and don't accept it as a valid means of communication. You'll come across many skeptics throughout your psychic and spiritual development journey. Many people will openly look down on you and speak negatively of your beliefs and practices. We're bringing this up because you can't let these voices get to you. If you doubt, for a second, that telepathy doesn't work, your efforts will be in vain. If you're vulnerable to criticism, it's best to keep your practices to yourself or talk about them only with people you trust until you're fully confident about your abilities. With that in mind, let's explore how to send telepathic messages to anyone, regardless of the distance.

Believe in the Power of Telepathy

The first and most critical step in successfully sending telepathic messages to others is to fully believe in the power of telepathy and trust in your ability to practice it effectively. You don't shop online unless you're sure you'll receive your order. You don't keep worrying if you'll get scammed as long as you're shopping from a trusted vendor. You should approach telepathy with the same mindset. Place your order and let it go.

Telepathy and other psychic undertakings are already beyond our basic human comprehension. Spirituality is much greater than us, so it makes sense that your mind won't get the job done if you're tentative about the whole process. Having doubts, whether you affirm them or not, slows down your ability to deliver a telepathic message to someone. To avoid any disappointment, you should make sure that you're 100% positive about telepathy and have faith in your power to send mental messages.

Keep a Calm Mind and Body

When practicing telepathy, your mind and body should be calm as they would be if you're practicing mindfulness or meditation. You have to be as relaxed and peaceful as you can be. You don't need to take a trip to the mountains or a secluded beach to be able to communicate with someone telepathically. Just choose a time and place where you usually feel safe and comfortable. Make sure you won't be disturbed for the duration of your practice. Some people like to mentally connect with others right before they go to bed. Make sure that your room is at the perfect temperature - not too hot that you feel uncomfortable or too cold that you feel bothered. It should be chilly enough that it feels nice to curl up in your blanket. Keep the room pitch-black to avoid any distractions and find comfort in the silence. This way, you'll be able to get in tune with your higher consciousness and focus solely on the telepathic process.

This may not necessarily work for you. Some people feel uneasy when it's too dark or feel sleepy as soon as they lie down on the bed. Explore your own likes and dislikes and experiment until you find your ideal setting and environment, whether it is a local beach, forest, or even a spot that gives you the perfect view of the cityscape.

Use the Power of Visualization

To send your message, visualize the person you wish to communicate with down to the tiniest detail. Picture them vividly and feel their presence with your senses. Engage all your senses in the process. Imagine their eyes and how it feels to look right into them. Inhale their scent and listen to their voice. Visualize them right in front of you. Look at them and tell them what you wish to say.

Imagine the process as if it were real. Feel yourself saying your message, whether it's an expression of love or just something that you wish to communicate. You can also ask them to call, text, or do anything else. Telepathic messages should also be sent with good and loving intentions. Avoid using it to send negative energy to a person.

Once you feel like you've told them everything you wish to say, draw a deep breath and smile slightly. Open your eyes when you're ready. Even though it will take you a bit of practice, telepathic communications should feel natural and come as easily as in-person interactions.

Basic Telepathy Exercise

Find a trusted partner to practice this telepathy exercise with, and follow these steps:

Step 1: Sit across from your partner around 1.5 to 2 feet apart. This distance should be intimate yet not too uncomfortable. Since you shouldn't cross your legs, your partner will not be right in front of you. Their legs should lie next to each other on the floor. Keep your hands locked together or folded to your chest.

Step 2: Look directly into each other's eyes without straining your vision. So instead of looking at them diagonally, keep your vision straight and just look at their right or left eye, depending on the side they're on.

Step 3: Now that you're focused on each other's eyes, you should both slowly expand your scopes of vision until you encompass each other's full faces. In a minute or two, the image of the other person's face will start changing. You'll experience increased blurriness. When this happens, tell your partner of this change. Don't go into any details. Just mention the intensity of this occurrence. Even though it seldom takes more than a couple of minutes, you should be open to the idea of spending 10 minutes doing this exercise if needed. This is because the human brain is trained to ignore any inconsistencies in its perception. The hardest thing about this exercise is finding the right words to communicate the changes in your vision as they undergo several levels of intensity.

Step 4: Each time you notice and communicate a change, verify that your partner is experiencing them at the same time and level of intensity. The stronger the changes, the more intense the visual alterations will be, so expect to feel overwhelmed and unsettled. You may need to take a break in order to regather your mental strength.

This exercise aims to train your mind to focus entirely on a certain action rather than your thoughts. Thoughts are highly subjective, so this activity aims to duplicate a similar level of subjectivity through an experience. Your mind will be too busy trying to see your partner's face clearly while staying focused on just one of their eyes. If you do this exercise correctly, you'll be too engaged to think.

Once you go past the stage of simple blurriness, the rest of the changes are hallucinatory. Your mind will be so surprised by the image you're seeing that it captures your full attention, generating even more intense hallucinations. If you start feeling uncomfortable, change your attention to something else or blink a few times.

"Eyes are the windows of the soul." Focusing on each other's eyes with this level of intensity gives you access to each other's consciousness. This means that when one of you is experiencing a hallucination, the other person is likely to experience it too. With practice, you'll be able to tell if what you're experiencing is a product of the other person's perception. When you notice that your partner is hallucinating, you'll naturally withdraw your visual concentration and will no longer duplicate your perception. Moving your attention from them will also cut off their hallucination.

The more you practice, the easier it will become for you to tune into other people's consciousness. All you'll need to do is focus on a person so you can duplicate their experiences.

Signs Your Telepathic Messages Are Received

Influence and Observe

If you're not willing to ask your partner or friend if they feel the urge to do something you want them to do, you can just watch their actions. Influence their thoughts by focusing on something that you want them to do.

Keep it simple. For instance, you can start thinking about your friend asking you to hang out. If they text you to ask if you're free without prior discussion of any plans, then they've received your message. Experiment often to make sure that it wasn't just a coincidence.

Your Friends Check on You

If you're facing a problem and start wondering if you should call them and ask for help, you may find them already calling you if you're telepathically connected. Your thoughts will travel to the right place, allowing you to receive help before you even ask for it. This can only happen with people you're very close and energetically attuned to.

They Dream About You

While this requires a higher level of telepathic skills, you can try to influence a person to dream about you. If you succeed, they'll probably tell you that they dreamt about you.

You Have Growing Similarities

If you're working on sending your thoughts to someone, you'll notice that you're both growing interested in similar things. If your friend mentions a place you want to go to or hums the melody of a song stuck in your brain, then your messages are being delivered.

Now that you've read this chapter, you can easily communicate with others telepathically. All you need to do is trust in the power of telepathy and your ability to do it successfully. With practice, you'll be able to send messages to people just by focusing your attention on them.

Chapter 8: Exercise Your Telepathic Muscles

Mind reading and telepathy only work if you fully control your will and can concentrate completely on something. Otherwise, your brain waves will be interrupted by many outside influences in the way, and you'll find it difficult to communicate telepathically. On that note, one should be well-versed in communication techniques as well as understanding other people's emotions and expressions. Only then can you be a successful telepath. Otherwise, you'll end up failing this task.

Mind reading and telepathy only works if you're in full control of your will and can concentrate completely on something.
https://www.pexels.com/photo/man-wearing-black-cap-with-eyes-closed-under-cloudy-sky-810775/

Now that you've learned both aspects of telepathic communication, you can finally put what you've learned into practice to send and receive telepathic messages. However, you can't expect to be a master mind reader just because you know the theory or techniques of developing telepathy skills. This unique skill requires a lot of practice, without which you'll just be another amateur mind reader who can't get it right. Although your effort may seem fruitless at the beginning, with consistent practice and concentration, you'll be able to accomplish wonders.

You've already gone through some basic techniques and scenarios to develop your mind-reading skills, but you won't become a master with a few techniques overnight. So, to help you further on this journey, this chapter is full of exercises and scenarios where you'll get to develop your telepathic skills with the help of some friends. Go through each exercise and apply it in real-life scenarios. Even if you aren't successful at first, after a while of practicing, you'll notice a marked improvement.

Before you start, create a harmonious energy or rapport between yourself and the person whose mind you're trying to reach. You can do this by meditation or rhythmic breathing, which you've already learned about in a previous chapter. Many people overlook this process step and end up making little to no progress in their telepathic journey.

It is important that you form a connection with the person you're trying to read so that a mental bridge can connect your mind. This is the best way to avoid any interference from other people's minds and only get through to the person you're communicating to telepathically. The stronger your rapport, the better you'll be able to communicate.

Finding Locations

To successfully carry out this practice, you'll need to guide your friend, let's call them the transmitter, to concentrate their will or thoughts while sending them toward your mind. It will then be your task to catch the signals being sent to you. Start this exercise by standing, blindfolded, in the middle of the room together with your transmitter. Ask the transmitter to mentally select one corner of the room without telling you which they have chosen.

They must then project their will into your mind by concentrating really hard. At this point, you must also have a completely passive and receptive state of mind. There shouldn't be thoughts clouding your brain lest they clutter your mind. After a moment has passed, you will feel yourself wanting to move in a particular direction; even though you have no sense of direction, your mind will work automatically toward moving to that location. You may not get this right the first few times, but practicing will make your intuition better and your brain sharper.

Finding Large Objects

The next exercise is to find large objects like furniture items in the room. Don't get impatient if these tasks don't seem too interesting at the moment, as they are just preparing you for future tasks you'll need to accomplish. Ask the transmitter to focus on a piece of furniture or any large object in the room and mentally guide you toward it. While doing this, they will also be responsible for guiding you away from bumping into obstacles as you'll be blindfolded. For instance, if the transmitter is mentally directing you toward a chair, it should send psychic signals for you to receive. Continue practicing this exercise until you can find every piece of furniture in the room. Repeat the same exercise to find small objects if you'd like a more demanding challenge.

Finding Hidden Objects

Once you've mastered how to find objects in a room, it's time to learn how to find hidden objects that only the transmitter knows about. Ask your friend to hide a small object like a key, watch or phone in a cabinet, under a book, or in some hidden space while you stay out of the room. Once they've hidden the object, you can come inside the room and be mentally directed toward the hidden object. For this practice, you don't need to be blindfolded, considering the object is not in your sight. The transmitter will need to guide you toward the object by giving mental instructions like "up," "down," "left," "right," etc. you'll need to let your mind become completely receptive toward their signals.

Finding a Person

This exercise should be done with more than one person, a minimum of three people other than you. Start by asking them to select the person they'll need to locate. Everyone except you should know who has been chosen. After this, start by finding the person's general location by letting your mind guide you. You should be getting telepathic signals from the others' thoughts regarding the location you need to be at. Once you've found the general location of the person you're supposed to find, you'll have an intuitive feeling about whether you're in the right or wrong place. Then, start moving according to the urges you get. After a few attempts of this exercise, this feeling will get stronger, and you'll be able to recognize it better.

Finding a Book

Ask your friend to select a book from a bookcase and then put it back, either in the same place or somewhere else. Then, use your telepathic skills to find out which book was selected. This process will be very similar to the finding small objects exercise, but people will be a lot more surprised at this feat. Make sure you keep your mind open to mental guidance from your friend's mind or try to reach into their mind to get guidance or information. Move along the bookcase while letting your intuition and telepathic abilities guide you, and you'll automatically know which book was selected.

The Floral Tribute

This practice, again, requires more than one person and a bouquet of flowers. Ask one of the people to choose a flower from the bouquet and pick another person they want to give the flower to. Let them discuss the name of the person who's getting the flowers while you stay out of the room, unaware of their discussion. Once they've decided, pick up the separated flower, and take the hand of the transmitter, i.e., the person who picked out the flower for someone else. By doing this, you'll be able to read their mind through contact telepathy and find out the person for whom the flowers are intended.

The Hidden Jewelry

Again, you'll need more than one person for this exercise. Ask them to hide a small piece of jewelry on the person of someone without letting you know. For this exercise, you will need to combine what you've learned from the previous exercises to find a person and then the object. First, let your telepathy guide you toward the person's general location and then toward where they've hidden the piece of jewelry.

The Reunited Couple

This practice requires more than four people to be present for better practice. The audience should select two people to be married and one person to officiate their wedding. They should stand in the middle of the room as if they were about to be married, with the parson standing between them while you stay out of the room. Once they've done this and get back to their places or seats, you will need to find each person and arrange them in the positions they took without you knowing. For instance, the bride should be in her place, and the groom and parson should be in their respective places. While this may sound difficult, once you practice this technique, you'll realize that it's simply a variation of the exercise where you had to locate a person.

Replacing the Pin

This practice is another jaw-dropping feat of telepathy. For this exercise, your friend should insert a pin somewhere on the wall. The place should be accessible and not out of sight. Once they've made an indentation or mark, they should remove the pin and hide it somewhere in the room. Now, you have to let your intuition guide your sense of direction, and first, find the pin and then the general location of the indent. Keep in mind that finding the pin will be similar to you finding a small object. Finding the indentation's location is the same as finding a specific location in the transmitter's mind. Once you've narrowed down the general location of the indentation, use your hands to feel around for the indent.

The Reconstructed Tableau

This practice also requires a number of people to participate. Ask them to form a tableau and take specific positions in the group. Once they've finished, they should go back to their original positions, and you can come back into the room. While this may seem difficult, it's nothing you can't accomplish with a little practice. You will be required to reconstruct the tableau and arrange everyone according to their spots in the tableau. If you're having trouble reading someone's thoughts, specify a single person as the transmitter and focus on their thoughts so you're not confused.

The Theft

This exercise requires someone to act as a thief and steal someone (the victim) else's piece of jewelry or cash. The thief should then hide the stolen goods somewhere around the room and return to their original position. Your task will be to identify the thief, find the object, and finally identify the victim, and then return their belongings to them. This exercise is yet another combination of the exercises you've previously learned.

The Murder and the Detective

This is a spectacularly impressive feat if you can achieve it. Ask your friends to designate the roles of murderer and victim among themselves. They should also select an object, such as a dagger or a murder weapon. The scenario will be something along the lines of a murder carried out by someone using a dagger, which is then hidden in the room by the murderer. The murderer also dumps the victim's body (sitting in a chair, standing). Finally, the murderer themselves will get into position somewhere in the room. Now, once you enter the room, locate in sequence: the dagger, the victim, and finally, the murderer.

The Mental Image

This exercise will help you send someone a mental image through telepathic communication. For this, you will need to connect your mind with your friend's or partner's mind. Once you've done this, try imagining a specific image, but don't tell them about it. This could be anything, but don't be too specific on your first try. For instance, don't send them an image of a TV show scene but instead stick with a simple image like that of a teddy bear. Then, ask your partner to open their minds to your thoughts and ask what they see. It is very possible that this practice will not be successful for a while because your partner may not be used to telepathic communication, but you may start to get real results after a while.

Mind reading is something many people don't believe is possible, but if we open our minds to the possibility of this concept, anything is possible. The most important part of mastering telepathy is the development of a strong mental connection and control over your thoughts. This can only be done with lots and lots of practice, which you will hopefully find interesting to do. You may get stuck while practicing some of these exercises, but don't get frustrated or lose hope because practice does make perfect.

Chapter 9: Heal through Telepathy

While telepathy is commonly known as a mind-to-mind communication tool, it can also be used for much more noble purposes. Sending restorative energy to others (psychic or telepathic healing) is a popular way of using telepathic gifts. A common bond between two people allows telepathy to exchange energy between the sender's and recipient's minds - which is how psychic healing is conducted. Empowered by a surge of positive energy, the recipient's thoughts will influence their body and mind to restore themselves to a healthy and balanced state. Telepathic healing can be used as a distant healing approach or in-person when the recipient prefers an energetic healing method that doesn't require a manual application. This chapter delves into the meaning and practices of telepathic healing, including different techniques, meditation exercises, and more. You'll learn how to direct healing energy towards those in need - especially if the person is already telepathically bonded to you.

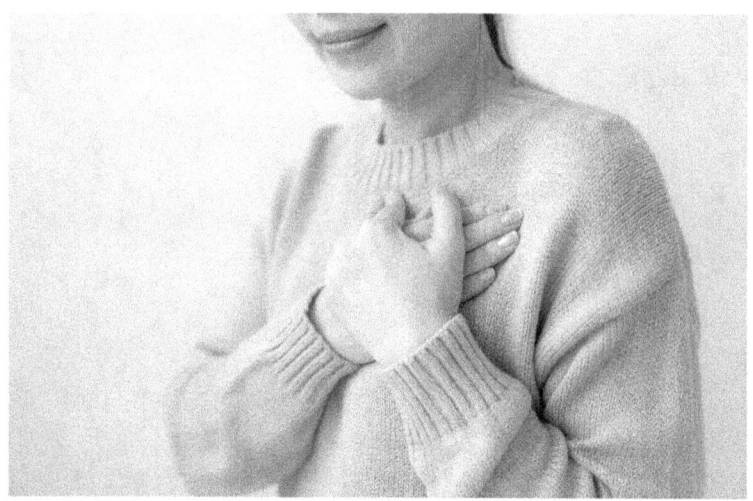

The Reiki distance healing method is one of the most common telepathic healing approaches.
https://www.pexels.com/photo/smiling-crop-woman-with-crossed-hands-5340278/

Telepathic Healing Exercises

The number of telepathic healing exercises is vast - and you may need to try a few before finding what works best for you and the people you're trying to heal. Here are some helpful telepathic healing exercises you can try.

Reiki Distant Healing

The Reiki distance healing method is one of the most common telepathic healing approaches. Developed by Master Usui, the founder of Reiki, distance healing is a specific and convenient technique for pain relief and the eradication of other symptoms. It can be applied anywhere, anytime - regardless of the physical location of the sender and the recipient. The patient doesn't have to do anything but be ready to receive the healing energy at the time indicated by the healer. They may be asked to relax their body and mind when they expect a burst of energy to come through and provide feedback about their state after receiving the power. The rest is up to the healer, who prepares their own body and mind for the session.

To perform Reiki distant healing, you should have a basic understanding of Reiki energy. This is essentially the same as psychic energy. It's the power that lies within you, allowing you to live a healthy and balanced life. You can manipulate it and channel it to where it's needed most to rebalance an energy point (chakra) or system in someone's body. This requires using Reiki symbols - written characters with a unique power of their own. One of the characters you'll need for distance healing is the Reiki Distant Healing symbol (Hon-Sha-Ze-Sho-Nen). This is often used combined with one or more empowering signs like Cho Ku Rei and Sei-He Ki.

Cho Ku Rei, the power symbol, is often used in distance healing in a traditional sequence called the Reiki Sandwich. While the arrangement in question can be used for other purposes, in this case, it consists of two empowering symbols and the distance healing symbol between them. Here is how to heal through this method:

- Write the recipient's name and the purpose of the energy transfer on a piece of paper. Fold and keep this paper in your hands, palms facing each other.
- Close your eyes and let your body and mind calm by focusing on your breath.
- Repeat the intention written on the paper, visualize Cho Ku Rei, and connect your psychic power to the energy of the symbol.
- Switch your focus to visualizing the distant healing symbol and picture it on top of or just beside Cho Ku Rei.
- Next, visualize another Cho Ku Rei symbol appearing on top or on the other side of Hon-Sha-Ze-Sho-Nen.
- Now that the Hon-Sha-Ze-Sho-Nen is backed up on both sides, you'll be able to send it to empower the recipient's energetic system.
- Focusing on your telepathic connection, you can start transferring the distant healing sequence into the recipient's mind, along with a boost of positive energy.
- Don't try to channel the energy toward a specific area. Telepathic healing is about sending the receiver positive and encouraging messages, so they can deal with their own issues.
- Visualize the healing energy enveloping your client and soak in every detail of your experience. You will want to share it with them in the future and compare it with their experience during the session.

After the energy transfer has been completed, let the client digest the new sensation for a few minutes or hours before inquiring about their experience and current state. If they describe feeling more relaxed than before, the positive energy has begun to take effect in their body or mind. Some clients may experience visions of certain activities, objects, events, or emotions. If they had something like this, see whether these were similar to what you've received. This will help you develop your telepathic abilities even more. If the recipients need any additional help in the future, you will already have a bond with them. This will make it easier to connect to them for healing purposes.

Healing through Telepathic Meditation

Whether you need to apply distance healing or not, meditation can be a great way to transfer positive energy. If someone calls you for telepathic healing, you can do a quick meditation exercise to help relieve their symptoms. Here is how to perform a psychic healing session through this method:

- Find a quiet space and get into a comfortable position. If the recipient is participating in a live healing session, you must ensure they are comfortable too.
- Ask them to take a few deep, relaxing breaths and do the same. If they aren't in the same room as you are, you'll need to consult with them first about the timing of the session. Tell them when you'll do it and how to relax as described above.
- When you're ready, close your eyes and focus on your telepathic connection with the person.
- Once you've ensured that the bond is strong enough, start concentrating on the problematic areas. For example, if they've complained about back pain, you start focusing on visualizing their back.
- Work on actively visualizing the positive energy reaching the person's mind and channeling it toward the affected area for 10-15 minutes.
- After that, take another deep breath, and disconnect from the recipient's energy. Slowly open your eyes as your mind returns to its own thoughts.

- Ask the recipient about their experience. Do they still feel the symptoms the same way? Has a new sign appeared?
- If they feel more energized, but some of their symptoms are still present, you should repeat the session as often as necessary.
- If a new symptom appears, you shouldn't continue healing the recipient, as this could be the sign that you're about to aggravate their condition.

Energizing the Upper Chakras

The chakra system is the primary recipient of healing energy. Each of the seven main chakras (also called energy points) requires a specific energy balance. However, the two upper chakras are the most sensitive to receiving positive energy. The crown and the third eye chakras are the recipients of the telepathic gift. They are responsible for distributing it toward the rest of the person's energetic system. They aid spiritual growth (both the healers and the recipients) - and can help the body and mind fend off diseases and heal from certain conditions. By energizing the crown and the third eye chakras regularly, you can create an effective energetic defense mechanism for the recipient. By establishing the communication between your upper chakras and the recipients, you'll be able to tap into their needs more efficiently. This will help you send clearer, more intuitive messages and share visions and other sensory signals that balance the chakras in question.

Here is how to balance the crown chakra:
- For this chakra, you'll need to meditate while visualizing or otherwise sensing the universal life entering your mind. You can do this before the session or anytime during the day when you need to sharpen your telepathic abilities.
- You can prepare for meditation with breathing exercises or yoga poses that affect the top of your head.
- If you are doing the meditation just before a healing session, the entire work should be performed at night. Preferably when the moon and the stars are visible in the sky.
- You can make this meditation part last as long as you need to feel your crown chakra re-aligned and ready to engage in

psychic energy transfer.

Here is how to balance the third eye chakra:

- The third eye chakra is highly spiritual. To balance it, you'll need to focus on your spiritual needs.
- Before your healing session, do a quick deep breathing exercise and follow up with a pose that increases blood flow circulation to the brain. You can find several yoga poses that fit this description. Or you can lie on the ground and put your legs up against the wall.
- Sit up, and begin your session by focusing on your third eye. Try to open it by visualizing or manifesting through any of the other clair senses.
- Listen to what your intuition tells you about healing the recipient in front of you. Let it help you manifest the best way to send positive energy.

Crystal Healing

Like Reiki symbols, crystals also have their own unique energy. As parts of nature, their power comes from nature's universal life force, which makes them a great tool in telepathic healing. If needed, crystals can also be charged with additional energy - whether it's yours or it comes from other natural elements, like the sun, the moon, or the spirits. Crystals can be combined with other psychic healing methods, such as telepathic meditation, affirmations, or any technique you prefer. The stones can be used one by one or set up in a crystal grid, which joins and concentrates their natural energy, making them even more powerful.

Depending on the level of healing required, crystals can provide the additional reinforcement you need to get the telepathic healing message across. Apophyllite, for example, is known to enhance psychic abilities. To use it during healing, follow these steps:

- Before your session, ensure you and the recipient are comfortable, relaxed, and undisturbed during the energy transfer.
- Take the crystal into your hands or wear it on your body as a charm during the session.+

- Take a deep breath and start gazing into the reflective surface of the stone. It will be the perfect tool for self-reflection - allowing you to see how powerful your psychic energy is.
- Let your mind relax and lose focus of your everyday preoccupations, and drift intuitively onto any thoughts or stimuli it wants to.
- Focus on the most positive thoughts or any thoughts that can tell you how to help the recipient through telepathy. You may receive guidance for healing and boosting your mental telepathy skills.
- Meditate or do a deep breathing exercise while keeping your connection with the crystal. Then, slowly start channeling the wisdom you collected toward the recipient, along with plenty of positive energy.

Past Life Regression Exercise

Past life regression is another healing approach that has gained popularity. And telepaths can make great use of it. It takes the patient beyond the experiences in their current life - and taps into the spiritual wisdom they've accumulated during their past lives. It involves getting a person into an altered state of consciousness (commonly known as a trance), during which they can access memories and experiences from other lifetimes. This helps the person understand themselves better. It also provides an opportunity to explore the recipient's personality traits, behavior patterns, potential health issues, and symptoms. All this can come in handy when trying to perform telepathic healing. Knowing how a person's soul has related to their environment in the past can give you a clue on how to channel the positive energy toward them so that they receive it as intended. Each past life is a surface on a person's multifaceted soul. You can obtain spiritual and personal growth and energetic healing by gaining awareness of each of them. Here is how to do a past life regression session:

- Start by getting both yourself and the recipient into a comfortable position. Get rid of all distractions, such as sounds and lights.
- Ask the recipient to close their eyes and relax their body. Prepare to send encouraging messages and positive energy through the sessions.

- Guide the person into a trance by asking them to calm their mind and focus on their breathing. They should take deep breaths until they feel their thoughts drifting away from everyday preoccupations.
- Advise them that they'll see a picture appearing - almost like a window opening in front of their eyes.
- Ask them to focus on light sources they can see appearing in their vision, as this will help them to see things more clearly.
- The picture should continue to widen and sharpen until they can make out individual details.
- Tell them to start moving in the space they see in their vision. Encourage them to open any doors or windows if they have these in front of them.
- Tell them to focus on what they can see when looking through the doors or windows they've opened. Are there any people in front of them? If yes, can they identify themselves with one of them?
- This will prompt them to discover their past soul selves and start exploring what that person did, thought, and felt.
- When they feel ready, they should slowly walk back to the initial point they saw when entering the trance and slowly start returning to the present.
- They may not find out much on the first attempt, but with enough practice, you can help them discover a lot about their soul.

Healing through Prayer and Affirmation

Prayers are well known for their healing effects. If the telepath and the recipient share similar beliefs, they can participate in prayer together. Or you can encourage the recipient to recite prayers by sending them positive energy. The prayers will elevate their spirit, and they'll be even more receptive to the healing energy. While prayers are often used as psychic healing tools for larger groups and communities, an affirmation can have the same effect on individual recipients. Both are great for distance healing because you aren't relying solely on your psychic power - but the power of their own mind to heal its energy. Positive affirmations are often used as a confidence booster and not necessarily a healing agent. However, a telepath can amplify the power of these positive messages. You can send them short affirmations through your telepathic gift and encourage them to repeat these daily. By prompting the recipients to recite positive affirmations frequently, you're creating an internal consistency within their minds that allows them to heal.

Tips for Telepathic Healing

As with any other telepathic practice, healing through telepathic energy requires at least two participants: you (the energy sender) and one or more recipients. While anyone can receive restorative powers, directing it toward them and ensuring it takes effect is sometimes a lot more challenging than it sounds. Apart from having a strong ability to tap into divine wisdom (which lies within you) and sending its power through time and space, you'll also need to be connected to the recipient. Just like people of many religions form a connection with the deities they follow and receive blessings and healing, you will need a strong bond between you and the recipient. Successful telepathy-receipt relationships are built on trust. So, as the first step, you'll need to reassure the recipient that you can tap into the source of divine energy and channel it to restore their energetic balance. Working in small steps and sending energy in small increments will allow you to show them you can contribute to their recovery. You can also form a connection that has nothing to do with healing, but it will give you more leverage. And when faith is established, their ability to receive the healing energy will improve even more, and their recovery will accelerate.

A telepath's subconscious can connect to the recipient's subconscious mind and heal their energetic system. However, permanent relief can only be obtained if the recipient's subconscious learns how to intuitively tap into its own healing energy. To do this, you'll need to form a powerful connection and send positive energy in a specific way by paying attention to the different channels. This takes plenty of time and practice to master - but it can be a life changer for people suffering from chronic conditions who need frequent relief and energy rebalancing.

Emotional bonds, while not always necessary, certainly help transmit healing messages. Because you are closer to your loved ones emotionally, you'll heal their energy through telepathy more quickly. The strongest bonds are between parents and children, siblings, and spouses - but even people in close romantic relationships or friendships can effectively heal each other. You'll also be more likely to feel their need for energetic healing, even without them telling you about it. While you should ensure you have their consent, getting permission to heal from a person you have a close relationship with will rarely be an issue. They'll already trust you. So, if you want to practice telepathic healing, the best way to start is with your loved ones. Tap into the energy of their mind and see if they need some help. If yes, send them a short burst of energy by focusing on the area they signaled they have issues with. Ask for their feedback. That way, you can see whether your techniques have worked or if you need to change something the next time you try helping someone through your psychic powers.

Disclaimers

The transfer of vicarious experiences can have an incredibly powerful effect on the recipient of the telepathic energy. Using your energy, you can balance out another person's spiritual energy, re-energizing them and helping them face their health challenges. That said, telepathic energy can't cure disease or injury. If the person who is seeking out telepathic healing suspects they have any physical or mental condition, they should consult a healthcare specialist regarding treatment. Once their doctor has established a diagnosis and conventional treatment plan, the patient can revisit the possibility of telepathic sessions as an additional therapy for their condition. If the person has already been diagnosed when they start considering telepathic healing, they should still consult their doctor regarding the combination of treatments. Their doctor should determine whether telepathy can be used in conjunction with conventional Western therapy. This is particularly true if the person suffers from a mental health condition. Undergoing telepathic healing can be an overwhelming experience, even for healthy minds. The messages can be confusing, and the energy can be too powerful. And if someone's mental well-being is not at its best, the session can do more harm than good. Other contraindications for receiving psychic therapy exist in patients suffering from seizures and certain heart conditions such as arrhythmia. Needless to say, you shouldn't perform telepathic healing if you aren't feeling well, either. This can affect the efficacy of your work - not to mention aggravating your own condition.

Make sure you always have the consent of the person you are trying to heal before you begin your session. Otherwise, they won't be receptive to positive energy. And by sending it, you could upset their energetic system even more. To avoid this, explain to the recipient what you're going to do and what they can expect from a telepathic healing session. Do this regardless of your chosen method and who you will be healing. This is a crucial step - and you shouldn't skip it even if the person is someone very close to you. Ask for consent before each session, even if they're already familiar with the procedure. If you're doing distant healing, call or text the person to ask for their permission before sending the energy. This will also allow you to ensure they'll be prepared to receive it.

Chapter 10: Raise Your Telepathic Protections

Regardless of what walk of life you come from, it's likely that at some point, you will encounter someone who just seems to drain all the energy out of you. These people are often called "energy vampires" because they seem to live off the positive energy of others. Energy or psychic vampires can be found anywhere, from the office to your own family. They come in all shapes and sizes and can equally be men or women.

What's more, energy vampires don't just suck your energy; they can also influence your emotions and thoughts. If you're not careful, they can even control you. So, how do you know if someone is an energy vampire? And what can you do to protect yourself from them? This chapter will explore those questions and provide you with some tips for dealing with negative energy.

Energy Vampires

At first glance, an energy vampire might seem like just another annoying or uncomfortable person. But, in reality, this term refers to someone who actively leeches away your energy, leaving you feeling exhausted and depleted. These individuals tend to be negative, manipulative, and self-centered, always focused on their own needs, and never willing to put effort into building genuine connections with others. If you find yourself repeatedly feeling drained after interacting with certain people, you may be dealing with an energy vampire.

While it can be difficult to deal with them, there are strategies you can use to protect yourself from their toxic influence. You may need to limit your time with them or simply set clear boundaries around what's acceptable and what isn't. Ultimately, having a strong sense of who you are and knowing when to say no is one of the best ways to keep yourself from being engulfed by an energy vampire.

Identifying Negative Energy

When dealing with negative energy, knowing where to start can often be difficult. Many people struggle with feelings of pessimism and negativity, but they may not be sure how to get out of that frame of mind. However, you can use a few simple strategies to identify and eliminate negative energy from your life. By staying alert to negativity and actively working to replace harmful thought patterns with more positive ones, it is possible to identify and counteract negative energy in your life.

1. Notice Mood Changes

When you notice changes in your mood or energy levels, examine the possible causes. For example, if you find yourself feeling more irritable than usual or experiencing a lack of motivation and your productivity is low, there could be something else at work besides just having a bad day or an illness. Negative energy can manifest itself in many different ways, and it is vital to recognize these changes so that you can take action as needed.

Whether it's avoiding certain people or places, seeking counseling, or simply pulling back from responsibilities for a while, noticing mood changes is an essential step toward treating whatever underlying issue may be the cause. Identifying negative energy allows you to take control of your life and pursue your true potential.

2. Check for Physical Symptoms

Recognizing negative energy can be difficult, especially when it is influencing your emotions or thoughts. However, some physical symptoms may also indicate the presence of this type of energy. For example, you may feel a general sense of heaviness or sluggishness while around someone with negative energy. Or you may notice that your mood suddenly takes a turn for the worse when interacting with this person. You could also start feeling unwell physically, experiencing headaches or stomachaches that seem to come out of nowhere.

By being aware of these physical symptoms and paying attention to them, you'll be better able to identify when negative energy is affecting your life and figure out ways to protect yourself from it. In the end, cultivating good energetic hygiene is essential to maintain mental and emotional well-being. And by becoming attuned to physical symptoms like those described above, you can stay alert and empowered in your efforts to guard against negativity.

3. Determine If There's a Pattern

When it comes to the presence of negative energy in your life, there can often be no clear indication. You may feel uncomfortable or uneasy without knowing why, or something that you once thought was positive may suddenly seem negative. However, some signs can indicate the presence of unwanted negative energy. For example, recurring bad luck or a general feeling of unease or pessimism can be signs that something is amiss.

Regularly experiencing physical manifestations (such as skin rashes or headaches) could also be manifestations of distress caused by negative energy. Ultimately, identifying and eliminating harmful negative energy from our lives is an essential step toward living happier and healthier. With awareness and intention, we can free ourselves from the negativity surrounding us and begin creating positive change in our lives.

4. Listen to Your Instincts

Whether you realize it or not, everyone is affected by negative energy. This can come in many forms, from toxic relationships and stressful work environments to bad habits and unhealthy lifestyle choices. Perhaps this is why so many people have learned to listen to their instincts, tuning in to their gut feelings as a way to identify and avoid negative energy.

Of course, this can be easier said than done. One of the keys to identifying negative energy is learning how to truly hear what your instincts are telling you. That means resisting the urge to dismiss or override those warning signs with logic and reason. Instead, try to be mindful of your emotions at all times, paying attention to cues like anxiety, stress, anger, or sadness as clues that something may not feel right. Additionally, take note of your physical reactions, ailments like headaches or stomachaches that crop up when you're around certain people or in certain situations.

If you notice any red flags, then it's time to take action and remove yourself from whatever situation is causing that negativity. Whether it's a toxic relationship that brings out the worst in you or a job that leaves you constantly exhausted and stressed out, responding proactively by listening to your intuition will help protect you from negative energy and keep you feeling balanced and happy. Ultimately, your instincts do know best!

5. Consider the Person's Actions

When we encounter people who seem to spread negative energy, it is natural to feel uneasy or anxious. This can be particularly true in larger groups or situations where it is difficult to avoid these individuals. But what does it mean when we talk about negative energy? In essence, this concept refers to how mean, spiteful, or harmful actions affect us physically, emotionally, and spiritually. While many people may dismiss such actions as mere "bad vibes," the truth is that negative energy produces very real effects. It can cause stress, depression, anger, and even physical illness.

So how do you identify the presence of this type of energy and manage its effects? One way is simply to consider a person's actions. If they seem motivated by selfishness or cruelty toward others, negative energy may be at play. By recognizing these behaviors and seeking support from loved ones and professionals when needed, you can break free from this toxic influence and live a happier life.

6. Get a Second Opinion

When it comes to identifying and dealing with negative energy, there is no better source than a second opinion. After all, often, another person has had the same experience and has the insight needed to spot anything that may be off or out of alignment. Whether you're trying to get clear in your situation or simply looking for someone else to bounce ideas off, getting a second opinion is a smart way to go. Not only will you get validation, and you'll gain greater clarity on any unsettling feelings, but you'll also benefit from the insights of an objective outsider who can explain what they and others are seeing from the outside. So don't hesitate to ask for help when it comes to dealing with negative energy. Get a second opinion and take control of your situation.

7. Look at the Big Picture

At first glance, it can seem as if negative energy is all around us. Whether we are dealing with toxic coworkers, stressful family situations, or overwhelming financial burdens, it can sometimes feel like there's no escape from the constant barrage of negative feelings and emotions. However, if we take a step back and look at the big picture, we can start to see that these negative experiences are just a small part of our lives. Likewise, we can begin to recognize that our ability to cope with these situations ultimately comes down to our attitudes and responses. We can learn to deal with it more effectively by cultivating resilience, positivity, and mindfulness in the face of negativity. At the end of the day, this may be one of the most vital skills that we have as humans; learning how to persevere through difficult times to come out stronger on the other side.

8. Identify Your Own Emotions

When it comes to emotions, it can be difficult to identify exactly what we are feeling. This is especially true when our feelings are negative or difficult to express. However, paying attention to our emotions and understanding why we are feeling a certain way is crucial. One of the best ways to do this is by observing the energy around us. Negative energy can manifest itself in many ways, from feelings of anxiety or depression to physical symptoms like headaches or difficulty concentrating.

By becoming aware of these signals, we can identify our negative emotions and take steps to address them. Whether that means changing our habits or seeking professional counseling, identifying our own issues is an essential first step toward managing our mental and emotional well-being. Start paying attention today. You never know what valuable insights may be lying just beneath the surface.

9. Educate Yourself about Gaslighting, Gossiping, and Fear-Mongering

If you're looking to improve your mental and emotional well-being, one of the best things you can do is learn about the different types of negative energy that exist in the world. This includes everything from gaslighting and gossiping to fear-mongering, all of which are designed to feed off our fears and vulnerabilities to lower our self-esteem and leave us feeling helpless and powerless.

The first step toward dealing with these negative forces is identifying them, as many people don't even realize this negativity is manipulating them. Next, once you see that a particular person or situation is working out in a toxic way toward you, it's crucial not to give them any further power or fuel through your thoughts and actions. Whether it's breaking free from an abusive relationship or maintaining strong boundaries with difficult people at work or in your personal life, remember that you always have the right to take care of yourself first by refusing to let others treat you with disrespect or abuse. Ultimately, this is the key to finding happiness, peace of mind, and success in all areas of life.

10. Pay Attention to the Language

As the saying goes, "Think before you speak." One of the vital skills that we need to develop as communicators is to pay attention to the language that we use when interacting with others. Whether we are having a face-to-face conversation or sending an email or text message, we must consider the energy and impact of our words. This means avoiding negative language and focusing our statements on positive and supportive messages. For example, instead of saying things like "You're always late" or "Everything you do is wrong," it's better to express your concerns in terms such as "I would appreciate it if you could be more punctual." By being mindful of our language, we can create more positive and uplifting energy that is good for everyone involved.

Dealing with Negativity

When dealing with negativity, get and stay grounded and keep a positive attitude. This can be difficult when faced with criticism or pushback, especially if the naysayers are loud or influential. However, remember that not everyone's opinion matters and that their negativity only reflects their insecurities or biases. With this mindset in place, you can confidently approach these challenging situations, focusing on your goals and priorities rather than worrying about what other people may think. By staying focused on the bigger picture and remaining true to your values, you can achieve success and rise above the negativity around you. In the end, that's what truly matters. Here are some more tips:

1. Raise Your Vibration

Raising your vibration is a big first step toward dealing with negativity. This can be challenging, especially when stressful situations or negative people surround us. However, you can control your state of mind no matter what is happening around you. One effective way to do this is through mindfulness exercises like meditation or deep breathing. These practices help calm the mind and bring your attention to the present moment, shifting your focus away from any negative thoughts or energies that may drag you down. By consciously cultivating positive energy within yourself, you can stay grounded and maintain a higher state of vibration, even in the face of negativity.

2. Create Healthy Boundaries

When it comes to creating healthy boundaries, one should know how to deal with negativity and hostility. Whether this comes from coworkers, family members, or even strangers, it's essential to have strategies to deal with negative energy in a calm, confident manner. Some key tools include staying grounded during challenging interactions, focusing on maintaining a positive attitude even if it feels forced, and knowing your limits and when you need to walk away.

By developing these skills and staying true to your values and priorities, you can create healthy boundaries around negativity that will allow you to flourish both personally and professionally. And remember that while others may try to pull you down, it's up to you whether they succeed or not. So always stand strong, stay positive, and create healthy boundaries.

3. Avoid Energy Vampires

If you want to lead a happier and more fulfilling life, avoid energy vampires, people, or situations that drain your positive energy and bring you down. These can be difficult to identify at first, as they often come in the form of seemingly innocent comments or activities. For example, a rude coworker may make snide remarks behind your back, sabotaging your professional reputation or the news may focus on all of the bad things happening in the world, making you feel overwhelmed and hopeless about your collective future.

Ideally, you want to distance yourself from these energy vampires to reclaim your power and stay focused on what is most important to you. One way to do this is simply by recognizing when negativity is swirling around you and being aware of how it may be affecting your emotions and daily activities. Ultimately, it's up to you to take back control of your life and resist falling into the trap of negativity. With a little patience and determination, you can easily conquer those energy vampires that stand between you and blissful happiness.

4. Be Proactive

As we go through life, it's inevitable that we'll encounter negativity from time to time. Negative attitudes can be deeply troubling and discouraging, whether it comes from our colleagues at work, our friends and family, or even strangers on the street. So how do we deal with negativity proactively and positively? The key is to approach these situations with care and kindness. Try to understand where the negativity is coming from, and take steps to defuse any tension or conflict before it has a chance to build up. You might also consider ways to shift your mindset so that you see negativity as an opportunity for growth rather than a source of frustration and anger. Being proactive in dealing with negativity can help you maintain your mental well-being while also keeping others happy and at ease.

5. Practice Forgiveness

To achieve peace and happiness in our lives, we must learn to practice forgiveness. Whether forgiving ourselves or others, letting go of negative emotions and feelings can be a crucial part of moving forward. Unfortunately, this can sometimes be easier said than done, especially when the negativity comes from difficult people or challenging situations. However, with time and patience, it is possible to learn how to deal with these situations in a way that feels authentic.

This may involve seeking out support from loved ones or practicing techniques like mindfulness or self-compassion. Ultimately, perseverance is key when learning to practice forgiveness. But when we eventually stumble upon success, the resulting feelings of relief and lightness will make all of the effort worthwhile. So, whatever your situation may be, remember that the benefits of forgiveness are always well worth the struggle.

6. Cut Energetic Ties

There are many options for cutting energetic ties and banishing bad vibes. Some people choose to burn sage or Champaka incense, which have cleansing properties that help purify the air and eliminate negativity. Others may prefer to use affirmations, repeating positive statements out loud until they sink in and take root in their minds. Still, others might find crystals helpful for absorbing and transmuting negative energies such as selenite or black obsidian. The key to banishing negativity is to align your thoughts with positive intentions and release any doubts or fears that might be holding you back. With a little practice, you can become a powerhouse of positivity and easily cut energetic ties with any unwanted negative energy.

7. Surround Yourself with Positive People

Living a happy, healthy life means surrounding yourself with positive people. This is because we are always influenced to some degree by those around us. If you are hanging around with folks who tend to focus on the negative aspects of any situation, you will find yourself doing the same. On the other hand, people who always seem to see the silver lining in any cloud can be an invaluable source of support and inspiration.

If you find that you are constantly surrounded by negativity and pessimism, there are certain steps that you can take to deal with this. First, try to understand why these individuals repeatedly bring you down. Are they going through difficult times in their own lives? Do they feel insecure or inadequate themselves? You will develop effective coping strategies by gaining a better understanding of what underlies this negativity.

We all need people in our lives who will challenge us and help us grow. So, if one or two members of your social circle routinely drive you crazy with their negative attitude, don't let this stop you from cultivating meaningful relationships with others. Instead, maintain balance and surround yourself with people who make you feel good about being alive. After all, what's the point of hanging out with other people if it isn't making your life better? The choice is yours. Choose happiness by surrounding yourself with positive people who believe in your abilities and celebrate your successes.

8. Visualize Happiness

Happiness is something that we all seek, and yet it can be surprisingly hard to find. This is especially true in today's fast-paced, often stressful world, where we are constantly bombarded with all sorts of issues, including negativity and difficulties. So how can we learn to visualize happiness amid the chaos of daily life? One key is to practice accepting everything that comes our way, both good and bad. This means seeing the bright side of things and understanding that setbacks and struggles are simply part of the human experience. By opening ourselves up to all aspects of life, both positive and negative, we can learn to appreciate every moment as a gift and stay focused on what truly matters most. And by doing so, we will start to visualize happiness every day.

To be a successful telepath, it is essential to raise your protective shields. This involves clearing your mind of distractions, focusing your thoughts on the task at hand, and building a strong mental barrier that can deflect any unwanted influences. There are many effective strategies for boosting your defenses, including meditation, visualization exercises, and affirmations. You may also want to incorporate other techniques, such as grounding and shielding crystals, into your routine to help reinforce your protective shields. With time and practice, you will successfully keep all outside forces at bay and ensure that only beneficial energies make their way into your mind. So, raise those shields, focus your mind, and hone your telepathic abilities today.

Conclusion

At first glance, the idea of telepathy may seem like something out of a science fiction novel or a magic trick. After all, how can mere thoughts or ideas be transmitted from one person to another, seemingly at will? In reality, telepathy is a scientifically proven phenomenon, and it has been the subject of numerous groundbreaking experiments in the 20th century. For example, researchers have found that certain individuals can regulate brain waves and send signals directly into the brains of others via stored mental images. They have also discovered that these signals can be amplified by transmitters and receivers and even used to convey messages – sometimes cross-country!

Though our understanding of this unique ability is still limited, it's clear that telepathy is not just something out of a science fiction story – it's real and waiting to be harnessed for all sorts of potential uses. Its potential is only limited by our imagination. Some people believe that telepathy may even be the key to unlocking other abilities, like precognition or clairvoyance. This easy-to-follow guide has informed you about everything you need to know about this fascinating ability, including how to develop your telepathic skills.

In this book, you learned about the history of telepathy and some of the groundbreaking experiments that have been conducted on this phenomenon. We also explored how meditation can help improve your telepathic abilities and some of the different ways you can use telepathy in your everyday life. You learned how to use telepathy to communicate with others, share messages and even heal yourself and others.

Raising your vibration and establishing a telepathic bond with others are essential steps in harnessing this ability, and we explored how to do both of these things. From there, we delved into the nitty-gritty of how to send and receive telepathic messages. Through practice and repetition, you can hone your skills and become a master of this ability. And finally, we looked at how you can use telepathy to heal yourself and others. The final chapter contains some essential tips on how to protect yourself from negative energies when using this ability.

Telepathy is a fascinating phenomenon that has long captured the imagination of scientists, artists, and everyday people alike. Despite centuries of skepticism and ridicule from those who don't believe in its existence, there is significant scientific evidence to support the claim that telepathy is real and scientifically proven. Even more impressive, this power can be developed and honed to infinite potential through repeated practice, yielding powerful results both for individuals and for society as a whole.

Just look at some of the incredible examples in recent history. Neuroscientists have used telepathic techniques to successfully treat post-traumatic stress disorder in veterans. Athletes have harnessed these abilities to improve their performance on the field, and ordinary people have used telepathy to connect with friends and loved ones across great distances. This ability holds tremendous potential for improving our lives and expanding our horizons.

Now that you've completed this book, you should have a good understanding of what telepathy is and how it works. You should also be well on your way toward developing your telepathic abilities. Whether it is clairvoyance, clairsentience, or any other form of extrasensory perception, remember to always use your abilities for good purposes. Telepathy is a powerful tool that can be used for both positive and negative purposes. It's up to you to decide how you will use it. So, what are you waiting for? Start practicing today and see what amazing things you can do!

Here's another book by Silvia Hill that you might like

Free Bonus from Silvia Hill available for limited time

Hi Spirituality Lovers!

My name is Silvia Hill, and first off, I want to THANK YOU for reading my book.

Now you have a chance to join my exclusive spirituality email list so you can get the ebooks below for free as well as the potential to get more spirituality ebooks for free! Simply click the link below to join.

P.S. Remember that it's 100% free to join the list.

~~$27~~ FREE BONUSES

- 9 Types of Spirit Guides and How to Connect to Them
- How to Develop Your Intuition: 7 Secrets for Psychic Development and Tarot Reading
- Tarot Reading Secrets for Love, Career, and General Messages

Access your free bonuses here
https://livetolearn.lpages.co/telepathy-for-beginners-paperback/

References

9 facts about telepathic communication. (n.d.). Operationmeditation.com. https://operationmeditation.com/discover/9-facts-about-telepathic-communication/

9 facts about telepathic communication. (n.d.). Operationmeditation.com. https://operationmeditation.com/discover/9-facts-about-telepathic-communication/

Demir, H. I. (n.d.). Quantum worlds from entanglement to telepathy. Fountainmagazine.com. https://fountainmagazine.com/2011/issue-84-november-december-2011/quantum-worlds-from-entanglement-to-telepathy

Grau, C., Ginhoux, R., Riera, A., Nguyen, T. L., Chauvat, H., Berg, M., Amengual, J. L., Pascual-Leone, A., & Ruffini, G. (2014). Conscious brain-to-brain communication in humans using non-invasive technologies. PloS One, 9(8), e105225. https://doi.org/10.1371/journal.pone.0105225

Hogan, B. (2021, August 19). Want to connect better with others? Practice telepathy to deepen your relationships. HelloGiggles. https://hellogiggles.com/what-is-telepathy/

Horowitz, J. (2016, May 31). 12 Powers You Didn't Know Professor X Has. ScreenRant. https://screenrant.com/powers-you-did-not-know-professor-x-has/

Lucia. (2019, July 1). How Zener cards work: ESP and the scientific method. The Ghost In My Machine. https://theghostinmymachine.com/2019/07/01/how-does-it-work-zener-cards-esp-and-the-scientific-method-karl-zener-j-b-rhine/

Mauro, C. (2015, July 9). Three types of telepathy. Reality Sandwich. https://realitysandwich.com/three-types-of-telepathy/

McRobbie, L. R. (2016, December 27). How one man used a deck of cards to make parapsychology a science. Atlas Obscura. https://www.atlasobscura.com/articles/how-one-man-used-a-deck-of-cards-to-make-parapsychology-a-science

Pruitt, S. (2018, October 17). The CIA recruited "mind readers" to spy on the soviets in the 1970s. HISTORY. https://www.history.com/news/cia-esp-espionage-soviet-union-cold-war

Siddhi, V. (2019). Iris publishers. Online Journal of Complementary & Alternative Medicine, 1(3), 1–4. https://irispublishers.com/ojcam/fulltext/is-telepathy-allowed-or-is-controled.ID.000515.php

Steinkamp, F. (2006). Telepathy: Or, How do I Know that this Thought is Mine? In Mind and its Place in the World (pp. 145–166). DE GRUYTER.

The biology of telepathy. (n.d.). Psychology Today. https://www.psychologytoday.com/us/blog/debunking-myths-the-mind/201804/the-biology-telepathy

What is the ganzfeld experiment? (n.d.). WebMD. https://www.webmd.com/brain/what-is-ganzfeld-experiment

Meditation for beginners - Headspace. (n.d.). Headspace.com. https://www.headspace.com/meditation/meditation-for-beginners

Shah, S., Ullman, S., & Ivanov, Z. (2022, June 17). 20 must-know meditation tips and techniques for beginners. Insider. https://www.insider.com/guides/health/mental-health/meditation-tips-for-beginners

Meditation: A simple, fast way to reduce stress. (2022, April 29). Mayo Clinic. https://www.mayoclinic.org/tests-procedures/meditation/in-depth/meditation/art-20045858

Walton, A. G. (2015, February 9). 7 ways meditation can actually change the brain. Forbes. https://www.forbes.com/sites/alicegwalton/2015/02/09/7-ways-meditation-can-actually-change-the-brain/

Aletheia. (2015, April 3). Do you have a "low" or "high vibration"? Read these 61 signs. LonerWolf. https://lonerwolf.com/low-or-high-vibration-signs/

MacLennan, C. (2018, January 12). 10 reasons to raise your vibration. Blissful Light. https://www.blissfullight.com/en-eg/blogs/energy-healing-blog/10-reasons-to-raise-your-vibration

Rebecca Joy Stanborough, M. F. A. (2020, November 13). What is vibrational energy? Healthline. https://www.healthline.com/health/vibrational-energy

What happens when you raise your vibration? (n.d.). Abundance No Limits. https://www.abundancenolimits.com/what-happens-when-you-raise-your-vibration/

Garis, M. G. (2020, July 28). How To Use Each of the 4 'Clair' Senses To Receive Information Psychically. Well+Good. https://www.wellandgood.com/psychic-clair-senses/

Burke, J. (2020, August 30). Psychic Senses - the clairs. Creative Empowerment. https://www.creativeempowerment.com.au/post/psychic-senses-the-clairs

Kelly, A. (2018, July 2). Am I Psychic? How to Tap Into Your Own Psychic Abilities. Allure. https://www.allure.com/story/am-i-psychic-how-to-tap-into-psychic-abilities

Lombardy, J., Lou, Kayla, Wille, & Balan, A. (2021, October 19). Clairaudience: What Is It & How To Develop This Psychic Ability. A Little Spark of Joy. https://www.alittlesparkofjoy.com/clairaudience/

Estrada, J. (2020, February 25). We're All a Little Psychic—Here Are 4 Ways to Develop That Intuitive Muscle. Well+Good. https://www.wellandgood.com/how-to-develop-psychic-abilities/

23 people tell the creepiest case of 'twin telepathy' they've ever witnessed. (2021, March 1). Thought Catalog. https://thoughtcatalog.com/emily-madriga/2021/02/23-people-tell-the-creepiest-case-of-twin-telepathy-theyve-ever-witnessed/

Brunton, S. (2022, April 29). How to spiritually connect with someone far away. Spiritual Unite; Kash and Susan. https://www.spiritualunite.com/articles/how-to-spiritually-connect-with-someone-far-away/

Fierro, P. P. (2008, June 12). Twin telepathy: Separating fact from fiction. Verywell Family. https://www.verywellfamily.com/twin-telepathy-2447130

Freid, L. (n.d.). Do twins really have telepathy? Psu.edu https://sites.psu.edu/siowfa14/2014/10/07/do-twins-really-have-telepathy/

Haddington, E. L. (2016, November 7). Five simple ways to connect with someone's energy. Soul and Spirit. https://www.soulandspiritmagazine.com/five-simple-ways-connect-someones-energy/

Harrison, P. (2018, January 25). 8 couples meditation exercises for you & your partner to experience. The Daily Meditation Coaching Sessions; The Daily Meditation. https://www.thedailymeditation.com/couples-meditations

Hogan, B. (2021, August 19). Want to connect better with others? Practice telepathy to deepen your relationships. HelloGiggles. https://hellogiggles.com/what-is-telepathy/

How to sense an energetic connection. (2019, January 12). Mike Sententia - A Scientist Explores Energy. https://mikesententia.com/2019/01/how-to-sense-an-energetic-connection/

Love, F. I. (2022, July 20). 5 couples meditation exercises to try with your partner. Keep the Romance Alive. https://www.freshinlove.com/33838/5-couples-meditation-exercises-to-try-with-your-partner/

Moheban-Wachtel, R. (2020, October 15). Three Easy Mindfulness Exercises you can do with your Partner to Strengthen Your Relationship. The Relationship Suite-Marriage & Relationship Counselor in New York City - The Key to Vibrant Long Term Relationships. https://relationshipsuite.com/three-easy-mindfulness-exercises-you-can-do-with-your-partner-to-strengthen-your-relationship/

Radford, B. (2018, March 27). The riddle of twin telepathy. Livescience.com; Live Science. https://www.livescience.com/45405-twin-telepathy.html

Stone, T. R. (2021, June 22). How does it feel when you connect with someone energetically? Inspired and free. Rose Colored Glasses. https://rosecoloredglasses.com/when-you-connect-with-someone/

Tantric Meditation for Couples [3 powerful stages explained]. (2019, August 1). Unifycosmos.com. https://unifycosmos.com/tantric-meditation-couples/

Twin telepathy: Does it exist? (n.d.). Teenink.com. https://www.teenink.com/nonfiction/academic/article/539371/Twin-Telepathy-Does-It-Exist

Watson, S. (2017, May 28). 19 twin telepathy stories that'll make you scream "oh, hell no!" BuzzFeed. https://www.buzzfeed.com/shylawatson/these-twin-telepathy-stories-will-shock-you

Hogan, B. (2021, August 19). Want to connect better with others? Practice telepathy to deepen your relationships. HelloGiggles. https://hellogiggles.com/what-is-telepathy/

Naicker, X. (2020, April 10). How to read minds in 4 easy steps (updated for 2022). Mysticmag.com; MysticMag. https://www.mysticmag.com/psychic-reading/how-to-read-minds-in-4-easy-steps/

PAIRS Foundation. (n.d.-a). PAIRS Mind-Reading exercise. Pairs.com. http://www.pairs.com/mind_reading.php

PAIRS Foundation. (n.d.-b). Shared meaning exercise for becoming a great listener. Pairs.com. http://www.pairs.com/shared_meaning_exercise.php

Scheucher, A. (2022, May 14). 13 ways to know if someone is sending you telepathic messages. Ideapod. https://ideapod.com/how-to-know-someone-is-sending-you-telepathic-messages/

Trespicio, T. (2017, November 7). Secrets of Communication from a Professional Mind Reader. MeQuilibrium. https://www.mequilibrium.com/resources/secrets-of-communication-from-a-professional-mind-reader/

Denisa. (2017, July 4). How to send telepathic message to someone you love or far away. Chi-nese.com. https://chi-nese.com/send-telepathic-message-someone/

Fey, T. (2021, November 24). How to know if your telepathic message was received. Ideapod. https://ideapod.com/how-to-know-if-your-telepathic-message-was-received/

Hogan, B. (2021, August 19). Want to connect better with others? Practice telepathy to deepen your relationships. HelloGiggles. https://hellogiggles.com/what-is-telepathy/

Annie Hanauer website. (n.d.). Anniehanauer.com. https://www.anniehanauer.com/annie-hanauer-projects/exercises-in-telepathy

Byng, A. (2022, June 20). What is Telepathy and 10 Ways You Can Practice it. Www.top10.com; Top10.com. https://www.top10.com/psychic-reading/what-is-telepathy-and-how-to-practice-it

Hogan, B. (2021, August 19). Want to connect better with others? Practice telepathy to deepen your relationships. HelloGiggles. https://hellogiggles.com/what-is-telepathy/

home. (n.d.). Home-ffm-tlv.com. from http://home-ffm-tlv.com/portfolio_page/telepathy-works/

Mauro, C. (2016, April 25). My practice: Spiritual telepathy. Spirituality & Health. https://www.spiritualityhealth.com/articles/2016/04/25/my-practice-spiritual-telepathy

StackPath. (n.d.). Mwrf.com. https://www.mwrf.com/technologies/systems/article/21158152/microwaves-rf-the-ultimate-personal-communication-method-perfected

The fourth lesson of telepathy - KSARS. (n.d.). Ksars.org. https://ksars.org/topics/the-fourth-lesson-of-telepathy

besguerra. (2019, May 28). Transmitting feelings—and healing—through telepathy. Lifestyle.INQ. https://lifestyle.inquirer.net/336556/transmitting-feelings-and-healing-through-telepathy/

Kamath, V. (2017, August 1). Power of Telepathy vs Artificial/Human Intelligence. Linkedin.Com. https://www.linkedin.com/pulse/power-telepathy-vs-artificialhuman-intelligence-vivek-kamath

LaBay, M. L. (2021, December 20). Everything You Need to Know About Past Life Regression Therapy. Linkedin.Com.

https://www.linkedin.com/pulse/everything-you-need-know-past-life-regression-therapy-mary-lee-labay

Luke. (2020, July 23). Reiki Distance Healing: Learn How to Send Healing Energy at a Distance. Thriveglobal.Com. https://thriveglobal.com/stories/reiki-distance-healing-learn-how-to-send-healing-energy-at-a-distance/

Mental Telepathy. (n.d.). HealingCrystalsForYou.Com. https://www.healing-crystals-for-you.com/mental-telepathy.html

BetterSleep. (2022, March 21). Chakras Explained: How to Keep Them Aligned. Bettersleep.Com. https://www.bettersleep.com/blog/chakras-explained-how-to-keep-chakras-in-alignment/

12 ways to recognize negative thoughts. (2019, July 15). Benevolent Health. https://benevolenthealth.co.uk/12-ways-to-recognise-negative-thoughts/

Cuncic, A. (2012, January 31). Negative thoughts: How to stop them. Verywell Mind. https://www.verywellmind.com/how-to-change-negative-thinking-3024843

Four ways to protect your energy. (n.d.). Kripalu. https://kripalu.org/resources/four-ways-protect-your-energy

How do you protect yourself from someone sending you telepathic messages? (n.d.). Quora. https://www.quora.com/How-do-you-protect-yourself-from-someone-sending-you-telepathic-messages

Identifying negative automatic thought patterns. (n.d.). Harvard.edu. https://sdlab.fas.harvard.edu/cognitive-reappraisal/identifying-negative-automatic-thought-patterns

Roncero, A. (n.d.). Automatic thoughts: How to identify and fix them. Betterup.com. https://www.betterup.com/blog/automatic-thoughts

www.ingramcontent.com/pod-product-compliance
Lightning Source LLC
Chambersburg PA
CBHW070339010526
44107CB00004B/551